collecting in cyberspace

A Guide to Finding
Antiques & Collectibles On-Line

by Shawn Brecka

Antique Trader Books
A division of Landmark Specialty Publications

ISBN: 0-930625-69-2
Library of Congress Card Catalog Number: 97-72623

Editor: *Allan W. Miller*
Editorial Assistant: *Elizabeth Stephan*
Designer: *Aaron Roeth*
Cover Design: *Jaro Sebek*

Printed in the United States of America

To order additional copies of this book or a catalog, please contact:

Antique Trader Books
P.O. Box 1050
Dubuque, Iowa 52004
1-800-334-7165

Antique Trader Books
A division of Landmark Specialty Publications

Contents

Introduction

The merging of antiques and collectibles and the Internet. Quite a concept. Some thought it would never happen, and others had no doubt. Today, what many thought, "remains to be seen," can be seen. As the Internet and other on-line services have become easier to use, many antiques and collectibles can now be seen floating about in Cyberspace.

Collecting in Cyberspace has been designed to help you better use the Internet and other on-line services and all of their vast resources that relate to antiques and collectibles. I have no doubt that this book will help connect you with other antiques and collectibles enthusiasts with whom you will buy, sell and trade; seek appraisals and the latest prices; and locate news and information in your areas of interest.

It amazes me how many antiques and collectibles sites are available on the Internet, although it probably shouldn't. Folks everywhere are embracing the Internet as a wonderful tool for hobbies such as antiques and collectibles. As more people jump on the bandwagon and become more technically proficient, the on-line antiques and collectibles areas will expand rapidly.

This book, however, is only a starting point. It is by no means a comprehensive listing of antiques and collectibles sites on the Internet, as new sites are popping up weekly, even daily. I've included as many sites as possible that include links to other sites so that you can link to a great many other places on the Internet than just those that are listed in this book. Also, since there is a lag-time between the gathering of data and the printing and distribution of this book, some of the sites will no longer be active or may have a different address by the time you're reading this. It's just one of the quirks about the Internet, but it shouldn't be too much of an inconvenience for you.

This book is written in a user-friendly way. By providing a broad overview of the Internet and on-line services before the primary section—The Phonebook—you can attain some of the basic knowledge you'll need to both understand and travel through Cyberspace. Following brief explanations about the most commonly used areas of the Internet and some terminology are guidelines for on-line purchasing and auctions. Next are directions on how to use some of the most popular on-line services, such as America Online and CompuServe. The phonebook, containing around 2,000 addresses, follows. I hope you enjoy this book as much as I enjoyed putting together.

Getting Started

To use the Internet or another on-line service, you need a computer, a modem, a telephone line and software. Most national on-line services, such as America Online and Prodigy, provide you with software. If you are using a local Internet provider, you will most likely need your own software for accessing the Internet, such as Netscape or Mosaic. These packages can be bought at nearly any software or office supply store, or you can usually get a free trial (shareware) version of software from the company itself, a friend or colleague. (If you get a trial version of software and decide to continue using it, you will need to purchase it.)

Your computer, along with the software, will use your modem and telephone line to connect to your Internet provider or on-line service provider. If you have call waiting, be sure to temporarily disable that service before using your modem—if you receive a call while using your modem, the "clicking" noise on the telephone line will interfere with data communications.

Speed is an important issue when talking about the Internet. There are several ways you can be more productive. When you are on the Internet, you are sending data back and forth. The speed of the modem refers to how fast it can transfer data. The speed is measured in bits per second, otherwise known as "baud." The higher the baud, the faster the modem. For instance, a 28,800 (28.8 K) baud modem is twice as fast as a 14,400 (14.4 K) baud modem.

If you're willing to sacrifice beauty for speed, turn off your graphics and load text only. The graphics on the Web are wonderful, but take lots of data—in other words, lots of time to transfer to your computer. Keep in mind that most local Internet providers will be faster than large national providers. This may not always be true, and you may want to compare. Even if your provider has 28,800 (or faster) connections, you may not actually be getting that speed from them, due to others also utilizing their service.

Once you are on-line (connected to your provider), let the surfing begin!

What is the Internet?

Simply put, the Internet is a collection of computers that are electronically linked together. Technically, it is a group of globally networked computers. Practically speaking, it is a resource for information and communication. As our culture becomes more technologically advanced, the Internet will become an increasingly important tool for information exchange. Will it be as important as the post office, the bank and the telephone? In my opinion, definitely.

The Internet can be used for communication, transferring information, entertainment, research, buying and selling, advertising, and the list goes on and on. Anyone can use the Internet, at any time. Everyone is welcome on the Internet, no one is excluded from its use.

What is E-mail?

E-mail (short for electronic mail) is a way to send and receive messages over the Internet. Your Internet service provider should supply you with your own e-mail address (for example, sbrecka@myprovider.com). E-mail can be used to send typed messages, programs, graphical images, newsletters and many other items to any other person who has e-mail.

What is the World Wide Web?

The World Wide Web, also known as "The Web," is probably the most talked about and utilized piece of the Internet. Graphics and text are used on the Web. The use of Hypertext allows point-and-click movement around the Web for a user-friendly atmosphere. For example, when you are reading something on the Web and notice certain words stand out (i.e., are a different color or are underlined), you can click on one of these words—called hypertext—that will link you to another place on the Web.

How To's

The following areas contain tips and advice on how to conduct business on the Internet:

Tips for On-line Purchasing

- If using a credit card for purchase, you need to decide whether or not to submit your credit card information over the Internet. There has been a lot of talk about the safety of doing this. In my experience, it's as safe as using it at a local store, telling it to a salesperson on the telephone or writing it on an order form that you mail. While this type of theft undoubtedly occurs, anyone desperate enough to steal your credit card information can find a much easier way to do it than become a computer hacker. Besides, there are also much bigger fish to fry.

- Most often, the buyer pays the shipping costs. But, this should be decided ahead of time between you and the other party, so as to avoid any confusion later.

- Some states require sales tax on mail orders and others do not. Some states require sales tax on shipping and handling charges, too.
- I've heard horror stories of people making purchases through the mail (or over the Internet). There are con artists and thieves out there; unfortunately, they are very good at what they do. One way to avoid this is to only do business with established firms or individuals. Keep a careful record of any transactions you make over the Internet or through the mail. If you do get burned, report it to the proper authorities.
- Don't be afraid to ask questions about the person you're doing business with. Ask for references. Ask for the names and phone numbers of other customers who you can contact. If you feel uncomfortable in any way about the person, don't do business with him or her.

On-Line Auction Tips

- Carefully read the rules for any auction you are considering participating in. These rules will tell you about how to bid, minimum bidding requirements, registration information, shipping and handling charges, payment terms, return policies and other pertinent information.
- Make note of the closing time and date of the auction (and pay attention to the time zone, too). Don't try to bid on an item in the last moments, since your bid may not arrive on time. E-mail takes more than just a second to reach its destination.
- You should be contacted at the end of the auction, either via e-mail or telephone, if you were the winner of an item. If not, there should be a place where you can check for prices realized.
- Many auction services allow you to place a "maximum bid." This service automatically increments your bid by a given amount up to a maximum that you set. For instance, if you bid $10 on an item and set your maximum bid at $20, the service will automatically increase your bid (by minimum increments) each time someone outbids you. The service will only bid for you up to the maximum pre-set bid.
- Most importantly, be a considerate participant in an on-line auction. Don't bid if you don't intend to buy. Also, pay particular attention to minimum bids and minimum increments.

Shipping and Handling

1. Before wrapping items for shipping, check them carefully. Make note of the condition of each item, and you should consider

taking photos for later reference. (Photos will help if making an insurance claim with the post office or other delivery service.) Check books for anything inserted between the pages, check clothing for anything in the pockets, check drawers for any items left behind and so on.

2. Select an appropriate sized box or shipping container. Make sure that there is enough room for the item(s) and all wrapping material necessary. Also check the box for proper strength and damage by water or greasy substances. If appropriate, consider using a padded envelope or other wrapping around the item (rather than using a box).

3. Wrap a first layer around each item carefully. Use tissue paper, plain brown paper, plastic bags or newspaper. Don't use anything with newsprint (such as newspaper) if this can rub off onto the item you are wrapping (such as on an old book or pictures). Also, don't use a bag that held food or items that leak (such as shampoo), as this may transfer to the item. Wrap each item separately. A container with a lid should have the top and bottom wrapped separately to prevent them rubbing against or bumping into each other during shipping.

4. Use some tape to wrap the first layer around each item. Items should be securely wrapped, but not too tightly. A very tight wrapping may cause strain on the item, particularly if the item is made of paper or can bend.

5. Use padding around items. Newspaper, brown wrapping paper, bubble wrap, packing "peanuts," or some other type of material should be used. Put some in the box first, then items to be shipped, and then fill the box with more packing material. This padding should be arranged to prevent items from shifting in the box and bumping into the edge of the box.

6. Tape up the box, making sure to tape along each seam that could pop open. It's also a good idea to cover the box with paper or plastic and tape.

7. Check the box to make sure that it is secure. Shake the box gently to ensure that the item(s) inside do not move or rattle around. If you do feel them shifting, open up the box and re-pack more tightly.

8. Write out the address label clearly onto a piece of paper (an index card works well) or directly on the box. Place clear tape over complete address on box. Then, write out your return address and tape over or affix it in the same manner in the upper left corner of the top of the box.

Getting Around: The Basics

Before setting foot into Cyberspace, you must have a basic understanding of what's out there, what you need to get there, and what you can do once you arrive. The following items should help:

E-Mail

E-mail is electronic mail. It is a system of using computers to exchange messages with others via computer networks. You can send e-mail messages to thousands of people around the world, to parents, friends, business associates and anyone else with an e-mail address. You need to use an e-mail package to access your e-mail account. Some common e-mail packages are Microsoft Exchange, Eudora and cc:Mail. Some Web browsers, such as Netscape, have e-mail retrieval systems built in.

Each person with e-mail has a personal e-mail address. These addresses are unique to each individual. The first part is the "userid" and the last part is the "domain name." The userid and domain name are separated by an @ symbol. For example: **sbrecka@myprovider.com**

Sbrecka is the userid and **myprovider.com** is the domain name. The proper way to say the previous e-mail address is: sbrecka at myprovider dot com.

The domain name tells where the e-mail user has an e-mail account. In the above example, the provider is "myprovider.com." If sending e-mail to someone on CompuServe, you need to use a comma (,) rather than a period (.) in the userid.

To send Internet e-mail is quite simple using your e-mail package or browser. First, address the message. Next, give the message a subject. Third, write the body of the message. Lastly, send the message.

Most people end their mail messages with a signature, a few lines of text containing their name and return e-mail. Additional information included in the signature may be phone number, street address and a quote. The majority of e-mail packages and browsers that support e-mail allow the user to set up a default signature that will automatically be placed on outgoing e-mail messages.

If you send an e-mail that is undeliverable, you will most likely have it returned to you with an error message. If this happens, you may have misspelled an address or perhaps the user is nonexistent (meaning that address does not exist on the server to which it was sent). If you misspelled the address, simply correct it and re-send the message. If you get the nonexistent error, check with the intended receiver to verify the address; if it was correct, he may be having difficulties on his end.

You may have occasion to run across mailing lists. These are systems in which messages are automatically e-mailed to everyone who subscribes to that list. Usually, anyone who subscribes to that list can also send messages to the list, in turn, sending a message to all the other subscribers on the list. Most lists are automated by mailing list programs. Some lists are moderated—this means someone filters through the messages before they are "broadcast" to all the subscribers of the list. By moderating the list, any unacceptable messages can be filtered out.

The World Wide Web

The World Wide Web, also known as WWW, W3, or the Web, is a hypertext-based information system. A hypertext document is one that includes links to other documents. Users of the Web can create, edit and browse Web pages. These pages provide a graphical interface to a vast amount of information.

To browse the Web, you must use a Web browser. Some popular Web browsers include Netscape, Mosaic and Microsoft Internet Explorer. With your browser, you can read the hypertext markup language (HTML) used on Web pages. These pages are "virtual" pages, in that they can be any size. Each page is created by the author to contain a "bite-size" chunk of related information.

Hypertext transfer protocol (HTTP) is used to transfer hypertext documents. Web page's addresses begin with "http" which tells your browser to use HTTP to retrieve the named HTML page. Most browsers also support file transfer protocol (ftp), and placing ftp before the address tells the browser to use ftp.

Web pages can include text, graphics, sounds, videos and links to other pages. A link is a word or item that, when clicked, will send you to another Web page or will download a file.

Web pages may sometimes ask you to select what version of Web page you want. For instance, it might ask whether you are using Netscape or Microsoft Internet Explorer. Browsers support different features, such as forms and tables. If your browser does not support the feature on the page, you may have difficulties viewing the page.

The uniform resource locator (URL) is an address for each page on the Web. In your browser is a place to put the URL. This is where you place the complete address (i.e., http://www.mysite.com). Most browsers (including Netscape and Internet Explorer) will assume the "http://" part of the address if you do not type it in.

You may run across sites that require a "helper" application. Helper applications are programs that remain in the background while you are browsing the Web and are utilized by your browser as necessary. Some helper applications include Macromedia Shockwave, Adobe Acrobat and RealAudio Player.

Browsing the Web and finding what you are looking for can be time consuming and confusing. Several sites have attempted to compile an index of the Web. These companies offer searches to help you find what you are looking for. The most popular of these can be found at:

http://www.altavista.digital.com
http://www.yahoo.com
http://www.excite.com
http://www.lycos.com
http://www.infoseek.com

To find sites specifically geared toward antiques and collectibles, try the following search sites:

http://www.curioscape.com
http://www.antika.com/collecting/index.html

Newsgroups

A newsgroup is a discussion group. Newsgroups are classified by subject. Articles—or messages—are posted to newsgroups by people with computers and newsgroup software. Anyone with access to a newsgroup can read the articles and respond. Most Web browsers support newsgroups. Some newsgroups are moderated, meaning that any article sent to the newsgroup gets filtered through a human moderator for approval before it becomes available for all to read.

You may hear the term "usenet" used to refer to newsgroups. Usenet refers to the entire system of newsgroups. Each individual newsgroup is dedicated to one subject, usually evident in the name of the newsgroup. For example, the newsgroup named **alt.autos.antique** deals with antique automobiles. Newsgroups are arranged into general categories as follows:

alt: alternative or informal
bit: Bitnet listserv mailing lists
biz: business related
clari: ClariNet
comp: computer science
news: newsgroups themselves
rec: recreation
sci: scientific research
soc: social issues
talk: debate & controversy
misc: anything else

The most-used groups for hobbies and recreation, such as those listed in this book, are the "alt," "rec" and "misc" groups. For a complete listing of all newsgroups available to you, your browser or newsgroup software should have an option to list them. Another way to get a list is to check out the newsgroup **news.lists**.

Some etiquette should be observed when participating in a newsgroup discussion:

- Do not post to inappropriate groups (for example, a question about Depression Glass in a pottery discussion group).

- Think before you post. If you are sending a personal message, or one that only a couple of participants in the group may be interested in, reconsider your decision to post. You can always use personal e-mail.

- When responding to or following-up another posting, give context to your reply by referencing the original posting. Use the minimum text necessary to do so and be sure to credit the right person.

- Read and edit your posting carefully before you post. Make sure your spelling and grammar are correct. Stay away from run-on sentences. Don't post test messages.

- When posting humorous or facetious comments, many people use a "smiley" or a "wink," but don't overuse them.

- Before asking a question, read the messages already in the group and read the group's FAQ, if it has one.

- If you believe someone has violated netiquette, send them a polite message by private e-mail. There is no need to "publicly reprimand" someone, and it may even get you into some trouble.

You may hear the term "flame" in reference to newsgroups. A flame is a message or article that contains strong criticism, usually derogatory or very emotional. It is best to avoid flaming. If you do get flamed, sit back and think before you respond. Most flames occur due to a misunderstanding. And if someone has offended you, and you do decide to respond, consider using private e-mail.

America Online (AOL)

America Online is an on-line service that also gives you access to the Internet. It provides its subscribers with a wide variety of data. The difference between America Online and the Internet is that you have to be a subscriber to America Online to access its data.

The first time you connect with AOL, you'll be offered the opportunity to learn about the system. You can select "Absolute Beginners," "AOL Basics," "AOL Essentials," "Match Your Interests," or you can opt out of this type of learning experience.

AOL is very easy to learn how to use. Its guided learning system is a good way to get started. Essentially, AOL uses keywords for fast moves around its system. First, you click on your "Keyword" button on the top of the screen, then type in the keyword you are looking for, then click on "GO." It's that easy.

America Online

There are many other things to learn about AOL and many other nice features. For the purposes of this book, using the keyword sequence discussed above is necessary. If you choose to use one of AOL's learning sessions, you'll learn a lot more about getting around AOL and customizing your account.

To get to the general area that includes antiques and collectibles, "Hobby Central," GO HOBBY. In this section is where you can then select antiques or collectibles. To get specifically to the antiques area, GO ANTIQUE. The easiest way to get to where you want to go quickly is probably to GO COLLECTORS. From here, you can select nearly any of the areas related to antiques and collectors—message boards, software and chat rooms. Message boards are just what they sound like, a place to post messages such as "want ads," "items for sale" or questions and answers. Software can be any files related to the topic. Chat rooms are meeting places to have live talks with others. There are some scheduled chat times that will be listed throughout this book in their appropriate categories.

CompuServe

To use CompuServe, first install its provided software. After completing the registration steps, you can connect with the service. CompuServe not only provides access to its own system, but also Internet access.

Getting around CompuServe is relatively easy. It uses a system of names that act as GO words. When you know the GO word for the area you want to go to, you simply select the SERVICES menu, and then GO. Next, type in your GO word and off you go! Another way to get the GO word prompt is to push CONTROL + G on your keyboard.

If you don't know what you're looking for, you can select FIND and type in a topic you are looking for. You'll receive a list of related services. You could also choose EXPLORE and search through various menus to find what you're looking for.

CompuServe

In this book, we'll be using GO ANTIQUES and GO COL-LECTIBLES most often. These areas have the vast majority of antiques- and collectibles-related message boards (forums) and chat rooms.

Prodigy

Prodigy is another on-line service. As a subscriber, you are provided with various data and Internet access. You need to be a subscriber to Prodigy to access its files. Unlike the Internet, Prodigy's files are not in the "public domain."

After installing Prodigy's software and completing the registration process, you may sign-on to its system. There are several ways to get around on Prodigy. You can use its menus and point and click your way to where you'd like to go. But the easiest way to get around is to JUMP. The A-Z INDEX is an alphabetical listing of key words that you can use to jump to each feature on Prodigy. To get to the A-Z INDEX, start your Prodigy software and type in "A-Z" in the field. Or you may prefer to open the GO TO menu at the top of the screen, once you are connected, and select A-Z INDEX. But, the easiest way to get the A-Z INDEX is to push F7 on your keyboard (once you are connected).

Once you know what key word(s) you need, select the GO TO menu at the top of your screen, then select JUMP TO and type in your key word(s). If you are using the A-Z INDEX, simply push <enter> or <return> with your key word(s) highlighted.

Related to antiques and collectibles, the key words to jump to are: COLLECTING, CONCOURSE, COLLECTING 1 BB and COLLECTING 2 BB.

Making Your Own Web Page

To make your own Web page for the Internet, you need to plan what you want on your page. Then, you need to make the page. Web pages are written in HyperText Markup Language (HTML). You can use a text editor or a program designed specifically for

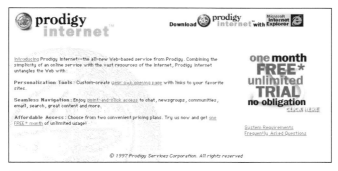

Prodigy

creating Web pages (such as Netscape Navigator Gold or Microsoft Internet Assistant). Don't be intimidated by making your own page—it's pretty easy. If you purchase a package for doing it, an instruction manual should be included as a guide. You can also search the Web for places that offer help or assistance. A great place to look for help is the NCSA Beginner's Guide to HTML located at http://www.ncsa.uiuc.edu/General/Internet/WWW/HTMLPrimer.html

After your page is created, you need a place to put it. Many local Internet providers will offer the service of "housing" your Web page. Additionally, national providers (such as America Online) offer this service. There is usually a charge for housing your page. After creating your page, give it a name and upload it to your provider's computer. After your page is available on the Internet, your last step is to simply tell everyone about it!

Disclaimer

Collecting in Cyberspace has been written to be as accurate as possible. While we apologize for any mistakes or errors within the book, author, publisher, agents and assignees cannot be held responsible for any error that may occur within the text of this book. Great care has been taken to check for accuracy of addresses and content descriptions.

Additionally, author, publisher, agents and assignees cannot be held responsible for computer viruses or other problems that the user may encounter by utilizing the Internet or any other on-line service provider. Any expenses or telephone charges incurred by use of the Internet or on-line service provider are the liability of the user. We recommend that you know the charges and fees of your provider and utilize a virus-checking program on your computer.

If you would like your site considered for inclusion in a future edition of this book, send the information to *Collecting in Cyberspace*, c/o Antique Trader Books, P.O. Box 1050, Dubuque, IA 52004-1050, or contact us on-line (see page 151).

The Phonebook

How to Read the Entries

Each entry in the book includes the name of the site and the address or instruction about how to locate the site. The Internet address is the "URL" that you type in to reach the site. If the site is on America Online, CompuServe or Prodigy, directions follow for how to get to the site. (Remember, too, that when you find a site you would like to return to at a later date, bookmark it.)

The phonebook listings may also include information about what is contained at the site. Here is an explanation of these items:

General Information: These sites contain information about that particular topic or could include exemplary descriptions of items.

Buy/Sell/Trade: This means just what it says—the site has items for sale, items wanted or items for trade.

Links: These sites have hypertext links to other sites.

FAQs: These sites contain answers to Frequently Asked Questions.

Auction: These sites have information about their auctions.

Price Guide: These sites have an on-line price guide for the antiques or collectibles in that category.

Link Sites

These sites include links to many other antiques and collectibles sites. Some of these sites are large directories of thousands of sites, and some have pages of links. They are handy sites for keeping up with new sites on the Internet.

Antique Alley
http://bmark.com/aa/index.html

The Antique Collectors' Internet Directory
http://www.connix.com/~tperry/index.html

Antique Hot Spots
http://www.antiquehotspots.com/

Antiques & Collectibles Guide
http://www.tias.com/amdir/amdir.html

Antiques & Collecting Newsletter
http://pages.prodigy.com/antique/

The Collector
http://www.prairienet.org/collector/

Collector Link
http://www.collector-link.com/

Collectibles by Nerd World Media
http://www.nerdworld.com/nw768.html

Collectors Emporium
http://www2.southwind.net/~vic/ds/cc_main.html

The Collectors Index
http://www.tdl.com/~k55k/

Curioscape
http://www.curioscape.com/

CyberMall
http://www.alpha-soft.com/cybermall/

From Here to Timbuktu
http://fromhere2timbuktu.com/links.htm

HandiLinks To Collectibles
http://www.ahandyguide.com/cat1/c/c80.htm

International Collectors Network
http://www.icn.co.uk/cat.html

International Memorabilia Dealers
http://www.wwcd.com/mrbl.html

The Internet Mall
http://www.internet-mall.com/

New Quest Ltd.
http://www.newquest.com/mall/

Nostalgia
http://home.sprynet.com/sprynet/gbond/nostalgi.htm

Super Expo Collectibles
http://www.superexpo.com/collect.htm

The World Shopping Mall
http://hudson.father.com/mall/

Victoriana
http://www.victoriana.com/

World Web Collectibles
http://www.wwcollectibles.com/

Auctioneers/Auction Houses/Auctions Sites

A-Mark Auction Galleries, Inc.
http://www.amark.com/amark

A & A Auction Company
http://web.wt.net/~aaa

A & A Auction Gallery
http://www.bonk.com/auctions

A.N. Abell Auction Co.
http://www.abell.com/auction

AB!C Absentee Auctions
http://www.netaccess.on.ca/~draaks/

Antique Marketplace
http://www.fred.net/dmaserv

AUCTIONnet
http://www.europa.com/auctionnet
Auctions-On-Line
http://www.auctions-on-line.com
Barridoff Galleries
http://www.biddeford.com/barridoff
Blackwood/March Auctioneers
http://www.webgarden.com/Blackmarch.html
Bonhams Auction House
http://www.bonhams.com
Brunson & Associates Auction Page
http://rampages.onramp.net/~zlajoie/auction.html
Burchard & Associates
http://www.auctions-fl.com
Byfield Enterprises, Inc.
http://www.byfield.com
Christies International
http://www.christies.com
Collectors Gallery, Inc.
http://www.ezlink.com/~lommerse
Coys of Kensington
http://www.coys.co.uk
Dan's On Line Auction
http://www.unm.edu/~mclind/antique.html
Dargate Auction Galleries
http://www.dargate.com
DeFina Auctions
http://www.csmonline.com/defina
Dorotheum Auction Houses
http://www.dorotheum.com
eBay's AuctionWeb
http://www.ebay.com/aw
Ehli's Auctions, Inc.
http://www.ehliauctions.com
ELA Auctions, Inc.
http://www.scruznet.com/~ela
Express Auction
http://www.expressauction.com/
Farley Enterprises Online
http://www.imall.com/farley
Gene Harris Antique Auction Center
http://www.csmonline.com/harris
The Great Gatsbys
http://www.gatsbys.com

Greg Manning Auctions
http://www.cluster.com/gma/auction
Hake's Americana & Collectibles
http://www.hakes.com
Harvey Clar Auctioneers & Appraisers
http://www.sirius.com/~javd/HarveyClar/Auction.html
Higgenbotham Auctioneers
http://www.higgenbotham.com
Iman Auction Company
http://www.csmonline.com/iman
Lunds Auction House
http://www.lunds.com/~lunds
Majestic Reflections Fine Art
http://www.majrefl.com
Manion's
http://www.manions.com/
Mroczek Brothers Auctioneers & Associates
http://www.halcyon.com/mba
Netis Auctions on the Web
http://www.auctionweb.com
NSA Auctions
http://www.mgl.ca/~nsa/main.htm
Olympic Auctions
http://www.infopost.com/olympics/index.html
Pacific Book Auction Galleries
http://www.nbn.com/pba
Phillips Auction House
http://www.phillips-auctions.com
Phoebus Auction Gallery
http://www.phoebusauction.com
Premier Auction Gallery
http://www.inf.net/~jcleary/premier.html
Redenbaugh Auction
http://www.redenbaugh-auction.com
Save The Earth Foundation
http://www.commerce.com/save-earth.html
Stamp Auction Central
http://www2.interpath.net/devcomp/auctions.htm
The Swapmeet
http://www1.primenet.com/amark
Theriault's
http://www.ea.net/theriaults
William Doyle Galleries
http://www.doylegalleries.com

World Wide Auctions, Inc.
  http://www.wwauction.com
Young Fine Arts Auctions, Inc.
  http://w3.maine.com/yfa
Zubal Aucton Co.
  http://www.zubal.com

Mall & Show Sites

These sites contain stores that sell antiques and collectibles from multiple sellers. The items that are the main focus of the dealers are listed.

Antique Addiction
  http://www.antiqueaddiction.com/homepage.html
  General Information, Buy/Sell/Trade, Links, Pictures
  Shops selling autographs, militaria, dolls, ephemera, coin-op machines, furniture, metals, sporting memorabilia, photographica, Western Americana

The Antique Explorer
  http://www.eden.com/~antexp/
  Buy/Sell/Trade, Links
  Shops selling arts & crafts, sporting memorabilia, metals, fine art, miscellaneous

Atlantique City Mega Show
  http://www.csmonline.com/atlantiquecity
  General Information
  The largest indoor antiques & collectibles fair in the world

Berkshire Antiquarian Book Fairs
  http://www.csmonline.com/babf
  General Information
  Book and ephemera shows

Collector's Super Mall
  http://www.csmonline.com/
  General Information, Buy/Sell/Trade, Links, Price Guide
  Shops sell just about everything; classified ads of items for sale and items wanted

Collector Online
  http://www.collectoronline.com/collect/
  General Information, Buy/Sell/Trade, Links
  Shops selling just about everything; classified ads of items for sale and items wanted

Dianne Vetromile: Curious Objects and Odd Stories
  http://www.diannevetromile.com/default.htm
  Buy/Sell/Trade, Links, Pictures
  Shops selling Occupied Japan, lamps & lighting, furniture, Art Deco, toys, miscellaneous

Facets Antiques and Collectible Mall
http://www.facets.net/facets/index.html
Buy/Sell/Trade, Links
Shops selling ephemera, glassware, Depression glass, limited edition, pottery/porcelain, miscellaneous

Heartland Antique Mall
http://206.21.6.249:80/antiques/home.htm
General Information, Buy/Sell/Trade, Links
Shops selling just about everything; classified ads of items for sale and items wanted

The Internet Antique Shop
http://www.tias.com/
General Information, Buy/Sell/Trade
Shops selling just about everything

Machine Age
http://www.cais.com/machine_age/index.html
Buy/Sell/Trade, Links, Pictures
Shops selling Art Deco, furniture, radios, ephemera; classified ads of items for sale and items wanted

Maine Antique Dealer Directory
http://www.mint.net/antiques.maine/
General Information, Buy/Sell/Trade, Links
Shops selling primitives, ephemera, photographica, dolls, toys, advertising, art, Disneyana, TV & movie memorabilia, posters, comic books, Western Americana, magazines, miscellaneous

Net Collectibles
http://www.netcollectibles.com/
Buy/Sell/Trade, Links
Shops selling just about everything

Palmer/Wirfs
http://www.csmonline.com/palmer
General Information
America's largest antique and collectible shows

Twice Told Tale Antique Mall
http://www.csmonline.com/twicetoldtale
Buy/Sell/Trade
Shops selling just about everything

General Antiques & Collectibles Sites

World Wide Web

4th Street Antique Gallery
http://www.csmonline.com/4thstreet
Buy/Sell/Trade
Featuring: everything!

20th Century Antiques and Collectibles
http://granite.koan.com/~pjones/
Buy/Sell/Trade, Links
Featuring: furniture, lamps & lighting, sporting memorabilia, miscellanous

A Little Store
http://www.corpsite.com/littlestore/home.htm
Buy/Sell/Trade, Links, Pictures
Featuring: advertising, dolls, ephemera, glassware, jewelry, kitchen collectibles, toys

American Antiquities
http://www.americanantiquities.com/
General Information, Buy/Sell/Trade, Price Guide
Featuring: art glass, automobile & farm machinery, artifacts, clocks, coin-op machines, furniture, lamps & lighting, jewelry, pottery/porcelain, music, rugs, toys

Americana Resources, Inc.
http://www.fred.net/ari
General Information, Buy/Sell/Trade
Featuring: everything!

American Pie Collectibles
http://www.ewtech.com/americanpie/
Buy/Sell/Trade, Links
Featuring: action figures, books, dolls, music, posters, toys

Antique and Collectibles Exchange Collectibles Exchange
http://www.worldint.com/ace/
General Information, Buy/Sell/Trade
Featuring: everything!

Antique Antics
http://www.antiqueantics.com/
Buy/Sell/Trade, Pictures
Featuring: glassware, jewelry, metals, pottery/porcelain

Antiquelane
http://www.antiquelane.com/
Buy/Sell/Trade, Pictures
Featuring: books, clocks, ephemera, furniture, glassware, jewelry, pottery/porcelain, primitives, toys, miscellaneous

Antique Networking
http://www.antiqnet.com/
General Information, Buy/Sell/Trade
Featuring: everything!

Antique Planet
http://rampages.onramp.net/~antiques/
General Information, Buy/Sell/Trade, Links, Pictures, Auction
Featuring: on-line auction of miscellaneous

Antiques & Elderly Things
http://www1.shore.net/~eldthing/
Buy/Sell/Trade, Pictures
Featuring: bottles, scientific & medical instruments, nautical, tools, Victoriana

Antiques Coast to Coast
http://www.csmonline.com/acrn
General Information
Featuring: everything!

Antiques from West Ridge
http://www.ncinter.net/~wrtiques/
General Information, Buy/Sell/Trade, Links, Pictures
Featuring: clocks & watches, country collectibles, furniture, lamps & lighting, pottery/porcelain, primitives, women's items, miscellaneous

Antiques of Vertu
http://www.metro.net/~tique/
General Information, Buy/Sell/Trade, Links, Pictures
Featuring: americana, glassware, metals, Orientalia, pottery/porcelain, miscellanous

Antiques-Resource
http://antiques-resource.com/pub/ANTQRESO.htm
General Information, Buy/Sell/Trade, Links, Auction
Featuring: everything!

ANTKonLINE
http://www.suba.com:80/ANTKonLINE/
Buy/Sell/Trade, Links, Pictures
Featuring: advertising, Art Deco, arts & crafts, '50s & '60s, pottery/porcelain, toys, World's Fair

Attic Antiques Online
http://206.21.6.249:80/antiques/dealers/attic/
Buy/Sell/Trade, Pictures
Featuring: advertising, Depression glass, glassware, kitchen collectibles, pottery/porcelain, women's items, miscellaneous

Auntie Q' Antiques & Collectibles
http://www.teleport.com/~auntyq/
General Information, Buy/Sell/Trade, Pictures
Featuring: advertising, Depression glass, glassware, holiday items, metals, ephemera, pottery/porcelain, miscellaneous

CamPro International
http://www.best.com/~campro/
Buy/Sell/Trade, Links
Featuring: action figures, books, G.I. Joe, magazines, militaria, sports cards, toys, trains

Candle Co. Antiques & Gifts
http://www.magic.mb.ca/~candleco/index.html
Buy/Sell/Trade, Pictures
Featuring: Coca-Cola, Wade, miscellaneous

Collectible Find Zone
http://www.li.net/~finders/index.html
Buy/Sell/Trade, Links
Featuring: books, dolls, ephemera, glassware, PEZ, toys, trading cards, miscellaneous

Collectibles in Paradise
http://www.aloha.com/~shakacat/
General Information, Buy/Sell/Trade, Links, Pictures
Featuring: Christmas collectibles, Hawaii-related, toys, jewelry, phonecards, pottery/porcelain, miscellaneous

Collectible Toy Mart
http://www.winternet.com/~toymart/
Buy/Sell/Trade
Featuring: die-cast, dolls, sports cards & memorabilia, toys, teddy bears, miscellaneous

Collective Past
http://web2.airmail.net/antiques/
Buy/Sell/Trade, Pictures
Featuring: dolls, jewelry, pottery/porcelain, primitives, quilts, textiles, toys

Collector's Collector
http://www.csmonline.com/collect1
Buy/Sell/Trade
Featuring: pop culture

The Collectors Network
http://www.footnet.com/collect/main2BAK.htm
General Information, Buy/Sell/Trade, Links, Pictures, Auction
Featuring: everything!

Collectors Super Mall
http://www.csmonline.com/
General Information, Buy/Sell/Trade, Links, Price Guide
Featuring: everything!

D'Antiques, Ltd.
http://www.dantiques.com/
General Information, Buy/Sell/Trade, Links, Pictures
Featuring: everything!

Doc and the Magic Lady
http://www.csmonline.com/doclady
Buy/Sell/Trade
Featuring: everything!

The Drawing Room of Newport
http://www.drawrm.com/
Buy/Sell/Trade, Links, Pictures
Featuring: ephemera, fine art, furniture, glassware, lamps & lighting, metals, pottery/porcelain, prints, textiles, miscellaneous

Durwyn Smedley Antiques
http://www.smedley.com/smedley/
Buy/Sell/Trade, Links, Pictures
Featuring: Art Deco, arts & crafts, jewelry, pottery/porcelain

Epage
http://ep.com/h/epages.html
Buy/Sell/Trade
Featuring: classified ads selling miscellaneous antiques & collectibles

Every Era Antiques
http://www.every-era.com/
General Information, Buy/Sell/Trade, Links, Pictures
Featuring: Art Deco, fine art, glassware, metals, Native American,
Orientalia, posters, pottery/porcelain, miscellaneous

Funk and Junk
http://www.funkandjunk.com/collectibles.html
Buy/Sell/Trade, Pictures
Featuring: advertising, books, lamps & lighting, magazines, metals, movie
& TV memorabilia, pottery/porcelain, sports cards & memorabilia,
tobacciana, toys, vintage clothing, miscellanous

Globalnet
http://www.mediaspec.com/GNET/
Buy/Sell/Trade, Pictures
Featuring: arts & crafts, clocks & timepieces, dolls, furniture,
photographica, scientific & medical instruments, sporting memorabilia

Golden Lion Antiques Mall
http://www.isomedia.com/homes/golden/default.htm
Buy/Sell/Trade, Pictures
Featuring: furniture, glassware, lamps & lighting, pottery/porcelain,
miscellaneous

Greystock, Ltd.
http://www.greystock.com/
General Information, Buy/Sell/Trade, Links, Pictures, Auction
Featuring: advertising, books, ephemera, fine art & antiquities, furniture,
lamps & lighting, prints, railroadiana

Hakes Americana & Collectibles
http://www.hakes.com/
Buy/Sell/Trade
Featuring: everything!

Hampton Roads Antique Connection
http://www.hrac.com/
General Information, Buy/Sell/Trade, Links, Pictures
Featuring: everything!

Harmening Haus
http://www.netins.net/showcase/hhaus/
Buy/Sell/Trade, Pictures
Featuring: clocks & watches, furniture, jewelry, vintage clothing

Highlander Antique Mall
http://www.hilndr.com/
Buy/Sell/Trade, Links
Featuring: advertising, automobilia, metals, pottery/porcelain, prints, tobacciana, miscellaneous

Hollyhock
http://www.golden.net/~mj/glassware.html
Buy/Sell/Trade, Pictures
Featuring: country collectibles, furniture, glassware, metals, pottery/porcelain, primitives, prints

International Collectors Network
http://www.icn.co.uk/cat.html
General Information, Links
Featuring: books, coins, ephemera, music, postcards, prints, stamps, toys, trading cards

Internet Arts & Antiques
http://www.wdsi.com/iaa/
General Information, Buy/Sell/Trade, Links, Pictures
Featuring: art glass, arts & crafts, lamps & lighting, limited edition, metals, pottery/porcelain, miscellaneous

Jack Black Enterprises
http://www.jackblack.com/
Buy/Sell/Trade, Links
Featuring: advertising, Art Deco, clocks, watches & timepieces, coins, jewelry, pottery/porcelain, primitives, toys, women's items, miscellaneous

Joe's Collectibles for Sale
http://pages.prodigy.com/jmccullar/collect.htm
Buy/Sell/Trade, Links, Pictures
Featuring: advertising, books, ephemera, toys, miscellaneous

John's Antique Mall
http://www.vividvision.com:80/~jwatts/antique.html
Buy/Sell/Trade
Featuring: books, comic books, fine art, ephemera, music, Native American, weapons

Journey's End
http://www.worldint.com/journeys/index.html
Buy/Sell/Trade, Links, Pictures
Featuring: Orientalia, limited edition, jewelry, pottery/porcelain, glassware, ephemera, toys, fine art, prints, miscellaneous

June Moon
http://www.collectors-row.com/june-moon/
Buy/Sell/Trade, Pictures
Featuring: action figures, pottery/porcelain, Star Wars, toys, TV & movie collectibles

Maloney's Resource Directory
http://www.csmonline.com/maloneys
General Information
Featuring: information on collectors, dealers, publications, auction houses and more

McIntosh-Weller Antiques
http://www.csmonline.com/mcintosh
Buy/Sell/Trade, Pictures
Featuring: everything!

Min's Antiques Intl
http://vru.com/mins/index.html
Buy/Sell/Trade, Links, Pictures
Featuring: art glass, limited edition, metals, pottery/porcelain

N&R Reflections Inc.
http://www.dnet.net/Russell/index.htm
Buy/Sell/Trade
Featuring: advertising, Art Deco, breweriana, dolls, glassware, limited edition, porcelain/pottery, teddy bears

Nana's Attic
http://www.nanasattic.com/
Buy/Sell/Trade, Pictures
Featuring: furniture, glassware, jewelry, metals, pottery/porcelain

Neatstuff and Collectibles
http://www.tsrcom.com/neatstuff/
Buy/Sell/Trade, Links, Pictures
Featuring: comic books, die-cast, magazines, posters, Star Wars, toys, trading cards

One of a Kind, Llc. Antiques...
http://www.connix.com/~tperry/index.html
Buy/Sell/Trade, Links, Pictures
Featuring: art glass, fine art, furniture, jewelry, metals, nautical, Orientalia, miscellaneous

Pacific Products Gallery
http://www.pacprod.com/gallery/collect.htm
Buy/Sell/Trade, Pictures
Featuring: animation art, Coca-Cola, country collectibles, pottery/porcelain, sporting memorabilia, TV & movie memorabilia, miscellaneous

Page Antiques, Fine Art & Collectibles
http://mindlink.bc.ca/Page_Antiques/
Buy/Sell/Trade, Pictures
Featuring: art glass, fine art, limited edition, metals, militaria, pottery/porcelain

Paper Collectors Mall
http://www.serve.com/ephemera/index.html
General Information, Buy/Sell/Trade, Links, Auction
Featuring: autographs, ephemera, magazines, trading cards

Pastimes Antiques & Collectibles
http://www.pastimes.com//
General Information, Buy/Sell/Trade, Pictures
Featuring: furniture, jewelry, photographica, postcards, sewing, miscellaneous

Pegasus Antiques
http://www.antiqueshop.com/
Buy/Sell/Trade, Links, Pictures
Featuring: Art Deco, clocks, watches & timepieces, Disneyana, glassware, jewelry, pens & pencils, pottery/porcelain, tobacciana, toys, vintage clothing, women's items, miscellaneous

Red Bow Antiques
http://www.csmonline.com/redbow
Buy/Sell/Trade
Featuring: Reprinted black Americana tobacco prints

SaskValley Antiques & Nostalgia
http://www.quadrant.net/antiques/index.html
Buy/Sell/Trade, Pictures
Featuring: arts & crafts, ephemera, pottery/porcelain, quilts, radios, sporting memorabilia, toys, textiles, miscellaneous

Something Olde
http://netnow.micron.net/~rbirk/index.html
Buy/Sell/Trade, Links
Featuring: books, Depression glass, glassware, limited edition, pottery/porcelain, miscellaneous

Spider's Web Antiques and Collectibles
http://www.nh.ultranet.com/~spider/
General Information, Buy/Sell/Trade, Links, Pictures
Featuring: advertising, ephemera, glassware, pottery/porcelain, miscellaneous

Sunset Pond Collectibles
http://members.aol.com/sunsetpond/index.htm
Buy/Sell/Trade, Links, Pictures
Featuring: jewelry, militaria, pottery/porcelain, toys, miscellanous

Super Expo Antiques Showcase
http://www.superexpo.com/antiques.htm
General Information, Links
Featuring: everything!

the-forum
http://www.the-forum.com/
General Information, Buy/Sell/Trade, Pictures
Featuring: everything!

Ventura Pacific Ltd.
http://www.fishnet.net/~sandcat/index.html
Buy/Sell/Trade, Pictures
Featuring: books, fine art, music, musical instruments, pottery/porcelain, teddy bears, toys, miscellaneous

Virtual Vintage
http://members.aol.com/rnjustin/vintage.htm
Buy/Sell/Trade, Pictures
Featuring: advertising, art glass, ephemera, furniture, glassware, jewelry, metals, pottery/porcelain, toys, vintage clothing, miscellaneous

Wilson Antiques and Collectibles Company Homepage
http://www.netins.net/showcase/antiquer/
Buy/Sell/Trade, Links
Featuring: advertising, Art Deco, books, breweriana, clocks, watches & timepieces, Disneyana, dolls, ephemera, furniture, glassware, pottery/porcelain, sporting memorabilia, TV & movie memorabilia, toys, miscellanous

World-Wide Collectors Digest
http://www.wwcd.com/
General Information, Buy/Sell/Trade, Links
Featuring: coins, comic books, sports memorabilia, stamps, Star Trek, toys, trading cards, trains

The World Collector's Net
http://www.worldcollectorsnet.com/
General Information, Buy/Sell/Trade, Links
Featuring: art glass, limited edition, pottery/porcelain

Related Publication Sites

Antique Trader Weekly
http://www.csmonline.com/antiquetrader/

Antiques and The Arts Weekly
http://www.thebee.com:80/aweb/aa.htm

Antiques, Art & Preservation
http://www.monka.com/antiques/

Art & Antiques
http://www.artantqmag.com/

Collect!
http://www.csmonline.com/collect/

Collecting
http://www.odysseygroup.com/collect.htm

Collector Magazine & Price Guide
http://www.csmonline.com/collectormag/

Collector's Mart
http://www.krause.com/collectibles/html/cl.html

Collectors News
http://collectors-news.com/

Every Era Antiques
http://www.every-era.com/

The Inside Collector
http://www.tias.com/mags/IC/InsideCollector/

Kovels
  http://www.kovels.com
The Maine Antique Digest
  http://www.maine.com/mad/
RETRO
  http://www.retroactive.com/
Today's Collector
  http://www.krause.com/collectibles/html/tc.html

Related Club/Association/Organization Sites

American Antiquarian Society
  gopher://mark.mwa.org/
Antique Collectors' Club
  http://www.antiquecc.com/
Antiques Council
  http://kiwi.futuris.net/ac/welcome.html
Collector Online Club Directory
  http://www.collectoronline.com/collect/club-directory.html
International Memorabilia Dealers
  http://www.wwcd.com/mrbl.html
the-forum
  http://www.the-forum.com/

Newsgroups

  rec.antiques
  rec.antiques.marketplace

America Online

Weekly Chat Session: Sundays, 9-10 p.m. ET
  GO COLLECTORS, select Chat Rooms, select Collectors Conference Room
General antiques & collectibles sites:
  GO ANTIQUE
  GO COLLECTING
  GO COLLECTORS

CompuServe

  GO ANTIQUES
  GO COLLECTIBLES
  GO NOSTALGIA

Prodigy

  Jump to COLLECTING CONCOURSE

Jump to COLLECTING 1 BB
Jump to COLLECTING 2 BB

Specific Categories Sites

Action Figures

<u>World Wide Web</u>

Action Figure Emporium
http://home.earthlink.net/~pilling/
General Information, Buy/Sell/Trade

The Action Figure Web Page
http://www.aloha.com:80/~randym/action_figures/noframes.html
General Information, Buy/Sell/Trade, Links, Pictures, FAQs

Action Figure Web Site
http://weber.u.washington.edu/%7Epredator/
Buy/Sell/Trade, Links

Action Figures and Collectible Toys (AFACT)
http://www.K-PGroup.inter.net/
Buy/Sell/Trade, Pictures

Action Figures Ring
http://members.tripod.com/~raulrdz2/
Links

Ancient Idols Collectible Toys
http://www.ewtech.com/idols/starwar.htm
Buy/Sell/Trade, Pictures

Arthur Hu's Toy Collecting Page
http://www.halcyon.com/arthurhu/collect.htm
General Information, Buy/Sell/Trade, Links

The Big Red Toybox
http://www.sky.net/~thomp64/
General Information, Buy/Sell/Trade, Links, Pictures, Auction

CamPro International
http://www.best.com/~campro/
Buy/Sell/Trade, Links

CR Toys & Collectibles
http://www.cet.com/~crtoys/
Buy/Sell/Trade, Pictures

The Curtis Action Figure & Collectable Page
http://members.aol.com/caumaug427/page1.htm
Buy/Sell/Trade, Links

D & S Sci-fi Toy World
http://members.aol.com/dnsroberts/index.htm
Buy/Sell/Trade, Pictures

IKE Action Figures & Playsets
http://home.stlnet.com/~ike01/toyindex.html
Buy/Sell/Trade

Lost in Toys
http://ng.netgate.net/~lostntoys/
Buy/Sell/Trade, Pictures

The Micronauts Homepage
http://www.carlow.edu/~elarse1/micront.html
General Information, Buy/Sell/Trade, Pictures

Monster's Collectibles
http://taz.interpoint.net/~monster/
Buy/Sell/Trade, Pictures

Nemesis
http://www.mtco.com/~nemesis/
Buy/Sell/Trade, Links

SpiffWare's Collectibles Marketplace
http://www.pagescape.com/fire/index.html
Buy/Sell/Trade, Auction

Toys Etc
http://pages.prodigy.com/toys_etc/toys2.htm
General Information, Buy/Sell/Trade, Links, Pictures

Related Publication Sites

Action Figure Digest On-line
http://www.tomart.com/
Action Figure Times
http://www.primenet.com/~btn/aft.html

Newsgroups

alt.toys.transformers
rec.toys.action-figures
rec.toys.vintage

America Online

Weekly Chat Session: first Wednesday of the month, 10-11 p.m. ET
GO COLLECTORS, select Chat Rooms, select Collectors Conference Room
Pangea Toy Network:
GO TOY

CompuServe

GO DOLLS, select action figures

Prodigy

Jump to COLLECTING 2 BB, select action figures

Advertising Items

World Wide Web

Antique Food, Cigar, and Seed Labels
http://www.sover.net/~oldlabel/
Buy/Sell/Trade, Pictures

Campbell Soup Company
http://www.campbellsoup.com/Welcome1.html
General Information, Buy/Sell/Trade, Pictures

Candle Co. Antiques & Gifts
http://www.magic.mb.ca/~candleco/index.html
Buy/Sell/Trade, Pictures

Coca Cola Buy/Sell/Trade Page
http://www.cocacola.com/trade/
General Information, Buy/Sell/Trade, Pictures

Collecting Sport Cereal Boxes
http://shopper.lv.com/Scott/collect.html
General Information, Buy/Sell/Trade, Price Guide

Collectric
http://www.collectric.com/
Buy/Sell/Trade, Links

CreatAbiliTOYS!
http://www.toymuseum.com/
General Information, Links, Pictures

Flake World
http://www.flake.com/
General Information, Buy/Sell/Trade, Links, Pictures

Harvey's Antique Advertising
http://www.nauticom.net/www/hbl/
Buy/Sell/Trade, Links, Pictures

Ken P's A&W Root Beer Mugs
http://www.islandnet.com/~kpolsson/mugs.htm
General Information, Pictures

Leonardo Park
http://www.hobbies.com/exhibit/advcoll/advcoll.html
Links

Mr. Peanut Collectible Page
http://chelsea.ios.com/%7Eosman/
General Information, Links, Pictures

Nabisco's Catalog of Gifts & Collectibles
http://shop.nabisco.com/
Buy/Sell/Trade, Pictures

OldToyDude's Toybox
http://members.aol.com/oldtoydude/toybox.htm
Buy/Sell/Trade

pepper.doc
http://www.swcp.com/~marbo/pepper.doc.html
General Information, Buy/Sell/Trade, Links, Pictures

Randy's Billboards of the Past
http://www.worldstar.com/~randy/
Buy/Sell/Trade, Pictures

Redzone Antique Firecracker Labels
http://www.sky.net/~redzone/labels/
General Information, Buy/Sell/Trade, Pictures

Rick's Gameroom Collectibles
http://www-opd.tamu.edu/~schulte/
General Information, Links, Pictures

Related Club/Association/Organization Site
Painted Soda Bottle Collectors Association
http://www.collectoronline.com/collect/PSBCA/PSBCA.html

America Online

Message Board:
GO ANTIQUE, select antiques & memorabilia A-L, select advertising collectibles

Prodigy
Jump to COLLECTING 2 BB, select Coke/Pepsi/bev

Ancient Artifacts

World Wide Web

Malter Galleries
http://members.aol.com/rarearts/malter/gallery.html
General Information, Buy/Sell/Trade, Pictures

Sadigh Gallery of Ancient Arts
http://www.iPGroup.com/sadigh/
Buy/Sell/Trade, Pictures

America Online

Message Board:
GO ANTIQUE, select antiques & memorabilia A-L, select ancient antiquities

Prodigy
Jump to COLLECTING 1 BB, select advertising memorabilia

Animation Art

World Wide Web
Animation and Fine Art Galleries
http://animationandfineart.com/
General Information, Buy/Sell/Trade, Pictures, FAQs
Animation Partners, Inc.
http://AnimationPartners.com/
Buy/Sell/Trade, Links, Pictures
Animazing Gallery
http://www.animazing.com/welcome.html
General Information, Buy/Sell/Trade, Pictures
The Cartoon Factory Online
http://www.cartoon-factory.com/home.shtml
General Information, Buy/Sell/Trade, Links, Pictures, FAQs
Cartoon Gallery
http://www.cartoon-gallery.com/
Buy/Sell/Trade, Pictures
CELMAIL
http://www.thegremlin.com/CELMAILhome.html
General Information, Buy/Sell/Trade, Links, Pictures
Great American Ink
http://www.gai-animation.com/
General Information, Buy/Sell/Trade, Links, Pictures
Rainbo Animation Art World Wide Web Connection
http://www.wenet.net/~rainbo/
General Information, Buy/Sell/Trade, Links, Pictures
Vintage Ink & Paint
http://www.vintageip.com/
General Information, Links
The Wonderful World of Animation
http://tribeca.ios.com/~debbiew/
General Information, Buy/Sell/Trade, Pictures

Art Deco

World Wide Web
Art Deco Collectibles
http://www.csmonline.com/artdeco
General Information, Buy/Sell/Trade
Antiques by Gallery 23
http://www.cyberconnect.com/gallery23/
Buy/Sell/Trade, Links, Pictures

Deco Echoes
   http://www.deco-echoes.com/
   General Information, Buy/Sell/Trade, Links, Pictures

Durwyn Smedley Antiques
   http://www.smedley.com/smedley/
   Buy/Sell/Trade, Links, Pictures

Lattimore's Global Art Deco Directory
   http://www.lattimore.co.uk/deco/
   Links

Related Publication Site

Lattimore's Global Art Deco Directory
   http://www.lattimore.co.uk/deco/index.html

Related Club Site

The Detroit Area Art Deco Society
   http://users.aol.com/daads/daads.htm

America Online

Message Board:
   GO ANTIQUE, select antiques & memorabilia A-L, select art deco

Art Glass

World Wide Web

Allan & Company Antiques, Inc.
   http://www.webinsights.com/allanantiques/
   General Information, Buy/Sell/Trade, Pictures

Black Bear Antiques
   http://homepages.together.net/~cbeaudin/
   Buy/Sell/Trade, Pictures

Eclectiques Carnival Glass & Collectibles
   http://www.qadas.com/eclectiq/
   General Information, Buy/Sell/Trade, Pictures

Page Antiques, Fine Art & Collectibles
   http://mindlink.bc.ca/Page_Antiques/page.htm
   General Information, Buy/Sell/Trade, Pictures

Robert Girard Gallery
   http://www.wdsi.com/isf/girard/
   Buy/Sell/Trade, Pictures

Severn's Art Glass & Collectibles
   http://home.earthlink.net/~bsevern/artglass.htm
   Buy/Sell/Trade, Pictures

Southern Belle Super Antique Mall
http://ourworld.compuserve.com/homepages/blacklig/southern.htm
General Information, Buy/Sell/Trade, Links
Wishful Things Art Glass & Antiques
http://www.bmark.com/wishfulthings.antiques/
Buy/Sell/Trade, Pictures
Woodsland
http://204.233.167.250/woodsland/carnivalglass/
General Information, Buy/Sell/Trade, Links, Pictures, Auction
Related Club Site
Fenton Art Glass Collectors of America
http://www.collectoronline.com/collect/club-FAGCA.html

Arts & Crafts

World Wide Web

Artisans
http://www.folkartisans.com/
General Information, Buy/Sell/Trade, Links, Pictures
The Arts & Crafts Society
http://arts-crafts.com/
General Information, Buy/Sell/Trade, Links
Fordham and Nelson
http://www.eden.com/~antexp/fnhead.html
Buy/Sell/Trade, Links, Pictures
J.R. Burrows & Company
http://www.burrows.com/
General Information, Buy/Sell/Trade, Links, Pictures

Newsgroup

rec.crafts.marketplace

America Online

Message Board:
GO ANTIQUE, select antiques & memorabilia A-L, select folk art
Message Board:
GO ANTIQUE, select antiques & memorabilia A-L, select arts & crafts movement

Autographs

World Wide Web

A & K Sports Collectibles
http://www.csmonline.com/aksports
Buy/Sell/Trade

Abacadabra Autographs
http://members.tripod.com/~SchlitzofPain/autographs
Buy/Sell/Trade

Al's Autograph Gallery
http://vanbc.wimsey.com/~jchim/autos.html
General Information, Pictures

Autograph Central
http://www.globalmall.com/autograph/
Buy/Sell/Trade, Pictures

Autograph Collectors
http://cscmosaic.albany.edu/~ss4569/autograph.html
General Information, Links, Pictures, FAQs

The Autograph Gallery
http://www.odysseygroup.com/odyssey.htm
General Information, Buy/Sell/Trade, Pictures

Autograph Online
http://www.io.org/~akennedy/
General Information, Links, Pictures

Autograph World
http://www.nh.ultranet.com/~jones/aw/
General Information, Buy/Sell/Trade, Links, Pictures

Autographics
http://www.entrepreneurs.net/autographics/index.html
General Information, Buy/Sell/Trade, Pictures, Auction

Autos & Autos
http://www.spunwebs.com/ads/spunwebs/autografpt1.html
Buy/Sell/Trade

Bailey's Autographed Sports Cards & Memorabilia
http://www.tc.umn.edu/nlhome/m598/bail0099/cards.html
Buy/Sell/Trade

Brian and Maria Green, Inc.
http://www.collectorsnet.com/cvdealer/bmg/bmginc.html
Buy/Sell/Trade

Celebrity Autographs
http://www2.csn.net/petrelle/autogrh.htm
Buy/Sell/Trade

Celebrity Autographs of Southern California
http://www.autographs.com/celebrity/
General Information, Buy/Sell/Trade, Pictures

Celebrity Connection
http://www.goodnet.com/~photos/
Links

Cheryl's Autograph Home Page
http://www.netcom.com/~cherylyn/autos.html
General Information, Links

Chip's Celebrity Home & E-mail Addresses
http://home.teclink.net/~chip1120/
General Information, Links, Pictures, FAQs

Cinemaholics
http://www.goodnet.com/~photos/cinema.htm
Buy/Sell/Trade

Comic, Fantasy & Gaming Card Autograph Collectors Home
Phttp://www.serve.com/ephemera/golees/artistautographs.html
General Information, Buy/Sell/Trade, Links, Pictures

Darryl's Home Page
http://www.kestrok.com/~darryl/
General Information, Links, FAQs

David Schulson Autographs
http://home.navisoft.com/schulson/index.htm
General Information, Buy/Sell/Trade

Deborah Perry Autographs
http://www.goodnet.com/~photos/perry.htm
Buy/Sell/Trade

Edward N. Bomsey Autographs, Inc.
http://www.clark.net:80/pub/rmharris/catalogs/bomsecat/intro.html
General Information, Buy/Sell/Trade

Frank J. Codispoti Memorabilia
http://www.ibb.com/fjcm.html
Buy/Sell/Trade

Fred Senese Autographs
http://www.goodnet.com/~photos/fsenese.htm
Buy/Sell/Trade

H. Drew Sanchez Autographs
http://www.goodnet.com/~photos/auto.htm
Buy/Sell/Trade

Hamilton's Book Store
http://www.gooooks.com/
General Information, Buy/Sell/Trade

Heritage Book Shop, Inc.
http://websites.earthlink.net/~heritage/
General Information, Buy/Sell/Trade

Historical Document Society
http://www.datacity.com/hds/
Buy/Sell/Trade, Links

Howard Schickler Fine Art
http://colophon.com/schickler/index_books.html
General Information, Buy/Sell/Trade

The Hump's Celebrity Address Page
Http://www.concentric.net/~thehump/auto.htm
General Information, Links

Justin G. Schiller, Ltd.
http://www.clark.net:80/pub/rmharris/alldlrs/ma/10022jus.html
General Information, Buy/Sell/Trade

La Scala Autographs, Inc.
http://home.navisoft.com/lascala/index.htm
General Information, Buy/Sell/Trade, Links

Lion Heart Autographs, Inc.
http://www.lionheartinc.com/index.htm
General Information, Buy/Sell/Trade

Man of Steal
http://www.csmonline.com/manofsteal
Buy/Sell/Trade

Moody's Collectibles, Inc
http://www.csmonline.com/moodys
Buy/Sell/Trade

My Autograph Page
http://www.aloha.net/~ritsn/autograph.html
General Information, Links

Nate's Autograph Hound
http://www.access.digex.net/~autohnd/
Buy/Sell/Trade, Links, Pictures

Paladins
http://www.goodnet.com/~photos/paladins.htm
Buy/Sell/Trade

Paper Collectors Mall
http://www.serve.com/ephemera/index.html
General Information, Buy/Sell/Trade, Links, Auction

Paul's Celebrity Autograph Web Site
http://www.magpage.com/~hunterp/
General Information, Buy/Sell/Trade, Links, Pictures

Ray's Primovera Cool-ectible's Catalog
http://www.access.digex.net/~yield/primo.html
Buy/Sell/Trade

Rivendell Rarities Ltd.
http://www.goodnet.com/~photos/rivndell.htm
General Information, Buy/Sell/Trade, Pictures

Rocky's Autographs & Memorabilia
http://www.goodnet.com/~photos/rocky.htm
Buy/Sell/Trade

Safka & Bareis Autographs
http://members.gnn.com/safka/index.htm
General Information, Buy/Sell/Trade, Links, Pictures

Sign Here...Autographs HomePage
http://www2.combase.com/~autographs/
Buy/Sell/Trade, Pictures, Auction

Signatures - Sports Autographs & Memorabilia
http://www.sportsmem.com/
Buy/Sell/Trade

Sportsnut
http://planet-hawaii.com/sportsnut/memora.html
Buy/Sell/Trade

Star Struck International
http://www.goodnet.com/~photos/starintl.htm
Buy/Sell/Trade

Tad's Celebrity Addresses Page
http://leahi.kcc.hawaii.edu/~adachi/address.html
General Information, Links

Thrill of Victory
http://www.csmonline.com/thrillofvictory
Buy/Sell/Trade

WHACO
http://www.erols.com/whaco1/
General Information, Buy/Sell/Trade, Pictures

Related Publication Sites

Autograph Collector
http://www.odysseygroup.com/acm.htm

Autograph Times
http://www.goodnet.com/~photos/at.htm

Sweet Spot
http://www.goodnet.com/~photos/sweetspt.htm

Trader's Horn
http://www.InstantWeb.com/t/thorn/home.htm

Newsgroup

alt.collecting.autographs

CompuServe

GO COLLECTIBLES, select autographs

Prodigy

Jump to COLLECTING 1 BB, select autographs

Automobiles

World Wide Web

American Classic Truck Parts
http://www.miraclemile.com/classictrucks/classtrucks.html
Buy/Sell/Trade

AMX Files
http://home.worldweb.net/~stoneji/amx.html
General Information, Buy/Sell/Trade, Links, Pictures

Antique Auto Traders On-Line
http://www.northernlife.com/northernlife/antiques/
Buy/Sell/Trade, Pictures

Auto Exchange Online
http://www.autophotos.com/index.html
Buy/Sell/Trade, Pictures

Automotive
http://www.vaxxine.com/aase/
Buy/Sell/Trade, Links

Automotive Web Index
http://www2.arnes.si/guest/uljfntfiz1/auto.html
Links

AutoPro
http://www.autopro.com/
General Information, Buy/Sell/Trade, Links, Pictures

Bill's Place in the Country
http://www.neca.com/~brauch/
General Information, Buy/Sell/Trade, Links

Blackhawk Collection
http://www.carnet.com/blackhwk/blackhwk.htm
General Information, Links, Pictures

Bombsight
http://www.geocities.com/MotorCity/1438/index.html
General Information, Buy/Sell/Trade, Links

The BumpStop
http://www.BumpStop.com/menu.htm
General Information, Buy/Sell/Trade, Links, Pictures

Calling All Cars
http://www.cacars.com/
General Information, Buy/Sell/Trade, Links, Pictures

The Car Junkie
http://www.esper.com/cltg/car.junkie/
Buy/Sell/Trade, Links

car lounge
http://carlounge.com/
General Information, Links

Cars & Parts
http://www.csmonline.com/carsnparts
General Information, Buy/Sell/Trade

cartalk.com
http://www.cartalk.com/
General Information, Buy/Sell/Trade

CATT Connection Online Classifieds
http://www.cattco.com/index.html
Buy/Sell/Trade

The Classic Car-Nection
http://www.car-nection.com/index.html
General Information, Buy/Sell/Trade, Links, Pictures

Classic Car Source Inc
http://www.classicar.com/home.htm
General Information, Buy/Sell/Trade, Links, Pictures, FAQs

Classic Firebird Page
http://www.jersey.net/~firebird68/birdpage.htm
General Information, Buy/Sell/Trade, Links, Pictures

Classic Motor Monthly
http://ourworld.compuserve.com/homepages/cmm_publications/
General Information, Buy/Sell/Trade, Links

Classic Mustang Page
http://www.vintage-mustang.com/
General Information, Buy/Sell/Trade, Links

ClassicNet
http://www.primenet.com/~komet/classic/clascars.html
General Information, Buy/Sell/Trade, Links, Pictures

Gilly's Auto Wreckers
http://spider.innercite.com/~ianjhunt/
Buy/Sell/Trade, Links

Hemmings Motor News
http://www.hmn.com/
General Information, Buy/Sell/Trade, Links

Highway One
http://highway-one.com/
Buy/Sell/Trade, Links, Pictures

Homepage DeSoto
http://www.desoto.org/welcome.html
General Information, Buy/Sell/Trade, Links

Hot Rods World Wide
http://www.america.net/com/hotrods/hrhome.html
General Information, Buy/Sell/Trade, Links

Iola Old Car Show
http://www.coredcs.com/~kfreiste/carshow/oldcarsh.htm
General Information

Land Yacht Marina
http://www.voicenet.com/~perches/landycht.html
General Information, Links

Minnesota Collector Cars
http://www.rawspace.net/thorf/cars.htm
Buy/Sell/Trade, Links

My Classic Car Online
   http://www.myclassiccar.com/
   General Information, Buy/Sell/Trade, Links, Pictures

Scott Stop USA
   http://www.csmonline.com/scottstop
   Buy/Sell/Trade

The Shelby Mustang Supersite
   http://www.netzone.com/~jamesk/shelby.html
   General Information, Buy/Sell/Trade, Links

The Swapmeet
   http://www.mm.com/swapmeet/
   General Information, Buy/Sell/Trade, Links

Thunderbird
   http://www.autopro.com/tbird/
   General Information, Buy/Sell/Trade, Links, Pictures

Vermont Auto Jumble
   http://www.sover.net/~autojum/
   Buy/Sell/Trade, Links, Pictures

vettes on the Net
   http://www.vannevar.com/USA/
   General Information, Buy/Sell/Trade, Links, Pictures

Wheels On-Line
   http://www.snsnet.net/wol/
   General Information, Buy/Sell/Trade, Links, Pictures

Related Publication Sites

AutoWeek OnLine
   http://www.autoweek.com/

Car Collector
   http://www.carcollector.com/

Cars & Parts
   http://www.csmonline.com/carsnparts/

Mobilia
   http://www.mobilia.com/

Old Cars
   http://www.krause.com/collectibles/html/oc.html

Old Cars Price Guide
   http://www.krause.com/collectibles/html/pg.html

Specialcar.Com
   http://www.specialcar.com/

Related Club Sites

American Motors Owners Association
   http://sciborg.uwaterloo.ca/~afleming/amo/amo.html

Antique Automobile Club of America
http://www.aaca.org/
International Thunderbird Club
http://www.autopro.com/ITC/
Jensen Healey Preservation Society
http://jensenhealey.com/
Mustang Club of America Inc.
http://www.mustang.org/
Nash Car Club of America
http://www.super-highway.net/users/nashclub/index.html
The National DeSoto Club
http://www.desoto.org/welcome.html

Newsgroups

alt.autos.antique
alt.autos.camaro.firebird
alt.autos.classic-trucks
alt.autos.rod-n-custom
alt.binaries.pictures.vehicles
rec.autos
rec.autos.antique
rec.autos.marketplace
rec.autos.misc
rec.autos.rod-n-custom
rec.autos.tech
rec.autos.vw
rec.toys.cars

America Online

Message Board:
GO ANTIQUE, select antiques & memorabilia A-L, select transportation memorabilia

Automobilia/Petroliana

World Wide Web

Automotive Collectibles BBS
http://pw1.netcom.com/~cramp/bboard.html
Buy/Sell/Trade
Chevron Exploration Zone
http://www.chevron.com/chevron_root/explore/index.html
General Information
Conoco Collector's Home Page
http://www.greenapple.com/~thelms/index.html
General Information, Buy/Sell/Trade, Pictures

Felix's Toy Truck Collection
http://members.aol.com/felixduke/toytruck.htm
General Information, Buy/Sell/Trade, Links, Pictures

Highlander Antique Mall
http://www.hilndr.com/
Buy/Sell/Trade, Links

Mobil
http://www.mobil.com/
General Information, Buy/Sell/Trade

Pennzoil
http://www.pennzoil.com/index.html
General Information, Buy/Sell/Trade

Primarily Petroliana
http://home.stlnet.com/~jimpotts/petroliana/index.html
General Information, Links

Shell
http://www.shellus.com/Welcome.html
General Information, Buy/Sell/Trade

Sinclair's Petroliana Page
http://www2.dtc.net/~sinclair/
Buy/Sell/Trade, Links

Speedway Motorbooks
http://www.primenet.com/~komet/speed/speedway.html
Buy/Sell/Trade, Links

Texaco
http://www.texaco.com/
Buy/Sell/Trade

Vermont Auto Jumble
http://www.sover.net/~autojum/
Buy/Sell/Trade

Related Publication Sites

PL8S Magazine
http://users.aol.com/pl8seditor/queen-b.htm/

Tiger Hightest Magazine
http://www.galstar.com/~hightest/

Related Club Site

Automobile License Plate Collectors Association
http://www.Charm.net/~shack/alpca.html

Newsgroup

alt.petromatica

America Online
Message Board:
GO ANTIQUE, select antiques & memorabilia A-L, select transportation memorabilia

Barbie

World Wide Web
Baddog's Groovy World
http://www.interlog.com/~baddog/
General Information, Buy/Sell/Trade, Links, Pictures, Auction

Barbie Collectibles
http://www.barbie.com/
General Information, Buy/Sell/Trade, Pictures, FAQs

Barbie Info
http://users.aol.com/barbie747/barbie.htm
General Information, Links, Pictures, Price Guide

Bear Essentials
http://www.thegrid.net/bear/bear.htm
Buy/Sell/Trade, Links, Pictures

Collectible Toy Mart
http://www.winternet.com/~toymart/
Buy/Sell/Trade

Deni's Vintage Barbie Collection
http://www.tir.com/%7Edavidson/
General Information, Buy/Sell/Trade, Links, Pictures

The Doll Attic
http://users.aol.com/sandihb4u/dollattc.htm
General Information, Buy/Sell/Trade, Links

Dolls, Gifts & More
http://www.wdsi.com/iaa/
General Information, Buy/Sell/Trade, Links, Pictures

DollWeb
http://www.cascade.net/dolls.html
General Information, Buy/Sell/Trade, Links, Pictures

Donna's Barbie Links
http://members.aol.com/DonnaM29/barbielinks.html
Links

JBJ's
http://www.jbjs.com/
General Information, Buy/Sell/Trade, Pictures

Kittie's Collectables
http://users.aol.com/kittyscol/kittys.htm
General Information, Buy/Sell/Trade, Links

Marl & B
http://www.auntie.com/marl/main.htm
General Information, Buy/Sell/Trade, Links

Meyer's Toy World New Barbie® Center
http://www.newbarbie.com/
General Information, Buy/Sell/Trade, Links, Pictures

MoonStar Creations
http://www.xmission.com:80/~aquadj/
General Information, Buy/Sell/Trade, Links, Pictures

P & D Collectibles
http://iaswww.com/pdgifts.html
General Information, Buy/Sell/Trade

Pippa's Barbie Page
http://www.servtech.com/public/pippa/barbie/
General Information, Buy/Sell/Trade, Links, Pictures, Price Guide

The Plastic Princess Page
http://d.armory.com/%7Ezenugirl/barbie.html
General Information, Buy/Sell/Trade, Links, Pictures, FAQs, Price Guide

Rose Gani
http://www.csmonline.com/gani
Buy/Sell/Trade

Totally Barbie
http://www.primenet.com/~jesica/
General Information, Pictures

Treasures & Dolls
http://www.antiquedoll.com/
Buy/Sell/Trade

Tricia's Barbie4Ever Page
http://pages.prodigy.com/Tricia.barbie/barbie.htm
General Information, Buy/Sell/Trade, Links, Pictures

America Online
Pangea Toy Network:
GO TOY

CompuServe
GO DOLLS, select Barbie

Prodigy
Jump to COLLECTING 2 BB, select Barbie

Bears

World Wide Web

Bear Essentials
http://www.thegrid.net/bear/bear.htm
Buy/Sell/Trade, Links, Pictures

Bear St.
http://www.pacificablue.com/bearst/
General Information, Buy/Sell/Trade, Pictures

Bears by the Sea
http://webmill.com/web/mill/bears/
General Information, Buy/Sell/Trade, Links, Pictures, Price Guide

Collectible Toy Mart
http://www.winternet.com/~toymart/
Buy/Sell/Trade

Good Bears of the World
http://www.wdn.com/jalbers/index.html
General Information, Links, Pictures

The Great Teddy Bear Hug Directory
http://www.teddybears.com/tgthome.html
General Information, Buy/Sell/Trade, Links, Pictures

GROWL House
http://www.growl.com/
Buy/Sell/Trade, Pictures

Gund
http://www.gund.com/
General Information, Pictures

Jennifer Martin's Teddy Bears & Collectibles
http://www.tyrell.net/~mobears/
General Information, Buy/Sell/Trade, Pictures

PAWS The Teddy Bear Shoppe
http://home.interhop.net/~paws/
Buy/Sell/Trade, Pictures

Treasures & Dolls
http://www.antiquedoll.com/
Buy/Sell/Trade, Pictures

Related Publication Site

Teddy Bear & Friends
http://www.cowles.com/magazines/mag/ted.html

Related Club Sites

Canterbury Bear Collectors Society
http://www.niia.net/~cbcs/cbcs.html

Good Bears of the World
http://www.wdn.com/jalbers/
Steiff Club
http://www.collectoronline.com/collect/steiff/steiff.html

Newsgroup
alt.collecting.teddy-bears

America Online
Pangea Toy Network:
GO TOY

CompuServe
GO DOLLS, select teddy bears
GO ANTIQUES, select dolls & teddy bears

Prodigy
Jump to COLLECTING 1 BB, select teddy bears

Bicycles

World Wide Web
The Classic & Antique Bicycle Exchange
http://www.tiac.net/users/cabe/
General Information, Buy/Sell/Trade, Pictures
Menotomy Vintage Bicycles
http://members.aol.com/Menotomy/index.htm
General Information, Buy/Sell/Trade, Pictures
Schwinn
http://www.schwinn.com/home/home_index.html
General Information, Pictures

Related Publication Site
The Classic and Antique Bicycle Exchange
http://www.tiac.net/users/cabe/

America Online
Message Board:
GO ANTIQUE, select antiques & memorabilia A-L, select bikes/pedal cars

Books (Collectible)

World Wide Web

A&B Books
http://ourworld.compuserve.com/homepages/jerry_vernon/
Buy/Sell/Trade

A-ha! Books
http://www.lightlink.com/tokman/
General Information, Buy/Sell/Trade, Links

A Sentimental Journey
http://www.rapidramp.com/Users/sjourney/
Buy/Sell/Trade

Aardvark the Antiquarian
http://www.aard-vark.com/
General Information, Buy/Sell/Trade, Links, Pictures

Abracadabra Booksearch International
http://www.henge.com/~abrabks/welcome.html
Buy/Sell/Trade, Links

Acorn Books
http://www.best.com/~acornbks/acorn.html
General Information, Buy/Sell/Trade, Links

Adder's Choice Bookstore
http://www.gsm.de/sf-books/
General Information, Buy/Sell/Trade, Links, Pictures

The Advanced Book Exchange
http://www.abebooks.com/
Buy/Sell/Trade

Alien Antiques
http://home.earthlink.net:80/~asimov/
Buy/Sell/Trade, Links

Annotators2 / Stina Enterprises
http://www.parkbooks.com/annotat2.html
General Information, Buy/Sell/Trade, Pictures

Antipodean Books, Maps & Prints
http://www.highlands.com/Business/Antipodean.html
General Information, Buy/Sell/Trade, Pictures

Antiquarian Book Network
http://www.antiquarian.com/
General Information, Links, Auction

Antiquarian Booksellers' Association of America
http://www.abaa-booknet.com/booknet1.html
General Information, Links

Antiques Network
http://w3.one.net/~dfi/
Buy/Sell/Trade

Any Amount of Books
http://anyamountofbooks.com/
General Information, Buy/Sell/Trade, Links

Arch Books
http://www.winternet.com/~archbook/
Buy/Sell/Trade

The Arkham Archives
http://www.primenet.com/~mael/
General Information, Buy/Sell/Trade, Links

Arlington Books
http://www.ArlingtonBooks.on.ca/
Buy/Sell/Trade

Artext
http://www.webcom.com/~artext/
Buy/Sell/Trade, Links

Asian Rare Books
http://www.columbia.edu/cu/ccs/cuwl/clients/arb/
General Information, Buy/Sell/Trade

Avid Reader
http://www.avidreader.com/
General Information, Buy/Sell/Trade

Baumgarten Books & Baubles
http://www.csmonline.com/baumgarten
Buy/Sell/Trade

Bibliofind
http://www.bibliofind.com/
Buy/Sell/Trade, Auction

Birds Nest Books
http://www.ism.net/~bnbook/
General Information, Buy/Sell/Trade, Links

Black Bird Books
http://www.cris.com/~blackbrd/
Buy/Sell/Trade

Blackstone & Coke Antiquarian Books
http://home.navisoft.com/blackstn/index.htm
Buy/Sell/Trade

Blake's Books
http://www.blakesbooks.com/
Buy/Sell/Trade

Book Gallery
http://home.interlynx.net/~websmith/book/book.htm
Buy/Sell/Trade

The Book Garden Gallery
http://www.eden.com/~bgg/
Buy/Sell/Trade

Book Look
http://www.macroserve.com/booklook/home.htm
Buy/Sell/Trade, Links

Book Mountain
http://www.booksused.com/
General Information, Buy/Sell/Trade, Links

Book Scout
http://www.angelfire.com/free/BookScout.html
Buy/Sell/Trade

Book Treasures
http://www.netanswers.com/bktreasures/
Buy/Sell/Trade

The Book Tree
http://www2.xh.net/~booktree/
Buy/Sell/Trade

The Bookcellar
http://www.bluemarble.net/~bookcell/index.html
Buy/Sell/Trade

Bookfinder's Book Mart
http://www.keytech.com/~ltiovan/
Buy/Sell/Trade, Links

BookMine
http://www.bookmine.com/
Buy/Sell/Trade

The Bookpress Ltd.
http://www.bookpress.com/
General Information, Buy/Sell/Trade

Books A to Z
http://www.booksatoz.com/
General Information, Links

Bookstream
http://www.bookstream.com/
General Information, Buy/Sell/Trade

Boston Book Company
http://www.rarebook.com/
General Information, Buy/Sell/Trade, Links

Brannan Books
http://redwood.northcoast.com/~brannanb/
Buy/Sell/Trade

Brilliance Books
http://members.aol.com/brillbooks/bookstore.HTML
Buy/Sell/Trade, Links

Broder's Rare and Used Books
http://members.aol.com/bookssss/index.html
Buy/Sell/Trade

Clayton Thompson - Bookseller
http://members.aol.com/Greatbooks/index.html
General Information, Buy/Sell/Trade, Pictures

Caduceus Books
http://www.io.com/~albion/cadu.html
Buy/Sell/Trade

Callaghan Booksellers, West
http://www.northlink.com/~books/index.html
Buy/Sell/Trade

Charles McKee - Books
http://mindlink.net/charles_mckee/homepage.htm
General Information, Buy/Sell/Trade, Links

Charles Parkhurst Books, Inc.
http://www.northlink.com/~books/chuck.htm
Buy/Sell/Trade

Christine Kovach, Bookseller
http://metropolis.idt.net/~kovach/
General Information, Buy/Sell/Trade, Links

Collectibles "Inc"
http://pages.prodigy.com/GMVY23A/search.htm
Buy/Sell/Trade, Links

CompuServe Book Catalogs
http://www.massmedia.com/~mikeb/
General Information, Buy/Sell/Trade, Links, Pictures, FAQs, Auction

D & D Galleries
http://www.dndgalleries.com/
General Information, Buy/Sell/Trade

David L. O'Neal Antiquarian Booksellers Inc.
http://www.tiac.net/users/onealbks/index.html
General Information, Buy/Sell/Trade, FAQs

De Kloof, Antiquarian Booksellers
http://www.xs4all.nl/~kloof/
Buy/Sell/Trade

Desiderata
http://www.desiderata.com/Books/index.html
General Information, Buy/Sell/Trade, Links

Directory of ABAA Booksellers
http://www.clark.net:80/pub/rmharris/alldlrs.html
Links

Edward J. Lefkowicz, Inc.
http://www.saltbooks.com/~seabooks/
General Information, Buy/Sell/Trade, Links

Fine Press Bookshop Online
http://165.247.199.4/finepress/
General Information, Buy/Sell/Trade, Links

Fireside Book Company
http://www.infinet.com:80/~fireside/
General Information, Buy/Sell/Trade, Links

Fred Hannah's Bookstore
http://www.adnet.ie/hanna/
Buy/Sell/Trade

Geiger's Books
http://www.geigers.com/
General Information, Buy/Sell/Trade, Links

The Gemmary
http://www.zweb.com/rcb/
Buy/Sell/Trade, Links

Gerry Kleier Books
http://www.bdt.com/home/kleier/
General Information, Buy/Sell/Trade, Links

Goldney Books
http://www.gold.net/users/ea48/
Buy/Sell/Trade

Gormley's Collectible Books
http://www.shore.net/~jerryg/
Buy/Sell/Trade

Hamilton's Book Store
http://www.gooxooks.com/
General Information, Buy/Sell/Trade

Heldfond Book Gallery
http://www.webcom.com/~bkgallry/
General Information, Buy/Sell/Trade, Links, Pictures, FAQs

Henry Hollander, Bookseller
http://www.hollanderbooks.com/
General Information, Buy/Sell/Trade, Links

Heritage Book Shop, Inc.
http://websites.earthlink.net/~heritage/
General Information, Buy/Sell/Trade

Hills Books
http://www.tricon.net/Comm/hill/
General Information, Buy/Sell/Trade, FAQs

Historicana
http://www.nauticom.net/users/judaica/Historicana/
General Information, Buy/Sell/Trade

Horizon Books
http://www.io.org/~errol/
General Information, Buy/Sell/Trade, Links

Howard Karno Books
http://www.cts.com:80/~karnobks/
Buy/Sell/Trade

Hugh Anson-Cartwright
http://www.interlog.com/~hac/
General Information, Buy/Sell/Trade, Links

The Ink Well
http://www.frii.com/~cce/inkwell/
Buy/Sell/Trade

It's a Mystery
http://www.mysterybooks.com/
General Information, Buy/Sell/Trade, Links

J & R Fine Books
http://www.crl.com./~rstorms/
General Information, Buy/Sell/Trade

J.R. Huber, Bookseller
http://www.tfweb.com/jrhuber/
General Information, Buy/Sell/Trade, Links

Janus Books Ltd. Online
http://janusbooks.com/
Buy/Sell/Trade, Links

John W Doull Books Online
http://emporium.turnpike.net/A/AAllen/jwd/jwda.html
General Information, Buy/Sell/Trade, Links

JP Books
http://jpbooks.com/
General Information, Buy/Sell/Trade, Links

Ken Spelman Rare & Antiquarian Books
http://dspace.dial.pipex.com/town/plaza/hi11/cover.htm
General Information, Buy/Sell/Trade, Pictures

L'Art Medical Antiquarian Books
http://www.xs4all.nl/~artmed/
General Information, Buy/Sell/Trade, Links

Last Word Books, Ltd.
http://www.register.com/lastword/
Buy/Sell/Trade

Louis Collins Books
http://www.halcyon.com/hannah/
General Information, Buy/Sell/Trade

Mark Seltzer - Books on Travel
http://www.interlog.com/~mseltzer/
General Information, Buy/Sell/Trade

Mark V. Ziesing / Bookseller
http://www.bigchair.com/ziesing/
General Information, Buy/Sell/Trade

Meyer Boswell Books, Inc.
http://www.meyerbos.com/
General Information, Buy/Sell/Trade

Michael John Thompson Antiquarian Bookseller
http://mindlink.net/Michael_Thompson/homepage.htm
General Information, Buy/Sell/Trade, Links, Pictures

Moe's Books
http://moesbooks.com/moe.html
General Information, Buy/Sell/Trade

Morrison Books
http://www.teleport.com/~morrison/
General Information, Buy/Sell/Trade

Muse rare and antique books
http://www.travel-net.com/~muse/
General Information, Buy/Sell/Trade

Nick's Books For Sale
http://www.users.interport.net/~papase95/sf/sfbooks.html
Buy/Sell/Trade, Links

Palm Tree Books
http://www.wco.com/~books/
Buy/Sell/Trade

Palmetto Presence
http://www.csra.net/21mall/ppresence.htm
General Information, Buy/Sell/Trade, Links

Pandora's Books
http://portal.mbnet.mb.ca/pandora/
General Information, Buy/Sell/Trade, Links, FAQs

Paper Moon Books
http://www.teleport.com/~paprmoon/
Buy/Sell/Trade, Links

Papyrus Books
http://www.PapyrusBooks.com/
Buy/Sell/Trade

Payson Hall Bookshop
http://www.tiac.net/users/payson/
Buy/Sell/Trade

Peter Bell Rare Books
http://www.gold.net/users/ad30/
General Information, Buy/Sell/Trade

Philadelphia Rare Books & Manuscripts
http://booknet-international.com/usa/prbm/
General Information, Buy/Sell/Trade

Powell's Books
http://www.powells.com/
Buy/Sell/Trade, Links

Randall House Rare Books
http://www.iinet.com/market/pia/randall/
General Information, Buy/Sell/Trade

Ray Boas, Bookseller
http://www.rayboasbookseller.com/index.htm
General Information, Buy/Sell/Trade, Links

Riverow Bookshop
http://www.mcs.net/~riverow/
General Information, Buy/Sell/Trade, Links

Robert Gavora Fine and Rare Books
http://www.teleport.com/~rgavora/
General Information, Buy/Sell/Trade

Rogue Books
http://www.autobahn.mb.ca/~parker/rogue/
Buy/Sell/Trade

Rulon-Miller Books
http://www.rulon.com/
General Information, Buy/Sell/Trade

Russell & Rutherford Antiquarian Books
http://members.aol.com/antiqubook/index.html
General Information, Buy/Sell/Trade

The Sacred and the Profane, Booksellers
http://www.cruzio.com/~profane/index.html
General Information, Buy/Sell/Trade

Sandcat Inc.
http://www.fishnet.net/~sandcat/index.html
Buy/Sell/Trade, Pictures

Scholars West
http://www.islandnet.com/~scholars/
General Information, Buy/Sell/Trade

Scribe's Perch
http://www.scribesperch.com/
General Information, Buy/Sell/Trade, Links, Auction

Second Story Books
http://www.paltech.com/secondstory/
General Information, Buy/Sell/Trade, Pictures

Significant Books
http://www.iac.net/~signbook/
General Information, Buy/Sell/Trade

Stone House Books
http://www.cris.com/~Shbooks/
Buy/Sell/Trade

Stray Books
http://ourworld.compuserve.com/homepages/StrayBks/
Buy/Sell/Trade, Links

Tall Tales
http://www.halcyon.com/msk/tlltales.htm
General Information, Buy/Sell/Trade

Tappin Book Mine
http://users.southeast.net/~tappinbm/index.html
General Information, Buy/Sell/Trade, Links, FAQs

Thaddeus Books
http://www.teleport.com/~symbol/thad.html
Buy/Sell/Trade

Therapeutic Bibliotheca
http://www.cybervision.sk.ca/hoff/books.html
General Information, Buy/Sell/Trade

Thomas G. Boss Fine Books
http://www.tiac.net/users/boss/
Buy/Sell/Trade

Ton Cremers and Marian Beereboom Books
http://www.GlobalXS.nl/home/c/cremers/
General Information, Buy/Sell/Trade, Links

Truepenny Books, Inc.
http://165.247.199.4/truepenny/
General Information, Buy/Sell/Trade, Links

UHR Books
http://mixnet.commdesign.com/~uhrbooks/index.html
General Information, Buy/Sell/Trade

Virtual Book Shop
http://www.virtual.bookshop.com/
General Information, Buy/Sell/Trade

Wesselman Books
http://www.xs4all.nl/~pwessel/books/#english
General Information, Buy/Sell/Trade, Links

William Matthews, Antiquarian Bookseller
http://www.vaxxine.com/matthews/
General Information, Buy/Sell/Trade, Links

Wonderland Books
http://www.dnai.com/~alland/
Buy/Sell/Trade

World Wide Wessex Books
http://www.donovan.com/books/wessex.htm
Buy/Sell/Trade, Links

Wrigley-Cross Books
http://www.teleport.com/~wrigcros/
General Information, Buy/Sell/Trade, FAQs

Related Club/Association/Organization Sites

Antiquarian Booksellers' Association
http://www.antiquarian.com/ABA/

Antiquarian Booksellers' Association of America
http://www.clark.net:80/pub/rmharris/booknet1.html

Antiquarian Booksellers' Association of Canada
  http://206.217.21.64/ca/index.html
Florida Antiquarian Booksellers Association
  http://www.antiquarian.com/FABA/
International League of Antiquarian Booksellers
  http://206.217.21.64/ilab/
Massachusetts & Rhode Island Antiquarian Booksellers
  http://www.tiac.net/users/mariab/
Provincial Booksellers Fairs Association
  http://www.antiquarian.com/pbfa/

Newsgroup
  rec.collecting.books

America Online
Weekly Chat Session: Wednesdays, 9-10 p.m. ET
  GO COLLECTORS, select Chat Rooms, select Collectors Conference Room
Book Collecting Area:
  GO COLLECTORS, select book collecting

CompuServe
  GO ANTIQUES, select books & prints

Prodigy
  Jump to COLLECTING 1 BB, select books & magazines

Breweriana

World Wide Web
The Beer Cap Page
  http://www.cam.org/~kibi/beercaps/capinfo.html
  General Information, Links
The Corkscrew Pages
  http://www.taponline.com/cork/cs.html
  General Information, Buy/Sell/Trade, Pictures
Corkscrew.Com
  http://www.corkscrew.com/
  General Information, Buy/Sell/Trade, Links, Pictures
Der Stein Haus
  http://www.sound.net/~stratton/
  General Information, Buy/Sell/Trade, Pictures
George's Tegestology Page
  http://www.millcomm.com/~brad/beer/
  General Information, Buy/Sell/Trade, Links

Kaiser Bill's
http://www.kaiserbills.com/
Buy/Sell/Trade, Pictures

Lou's Breweriana Unlimited
http://www.itw.com:80/lousbrew/
General Information, Buy/Sell/Trade

Pacific Coast Breweriana
http://www.netadventure.com/~pacific/
General Information

www.breweriana.com
http://www.breweriana.com/
General Information, Buy/Sell/Trade, Links

Related Publication Site
Canadian Bottle Magazine
http://www.netaccess.on.ca/~draaks/bottlemag.html

Related Club/Association/Organization Sites
The Association of Bottled Beer Collectors
http://ourworld.compuserve.com/homepages/John_Mann/abbchome.htm
Beer Can Collectors of America
http://www.itw.com:80/lousbrew/
Stein Collectors International, Inc.
http://www.paterson.k12.nj.us/~steins/

Newsgroup
alt.collecting.breweriana

America Online
Weekly Chat Session: first Thursday of the month, 9-10 p.m. ET
GO COLLECTORS, select Chat Rooms, select Collectors Conference Room
Message Board:
GO ANTIQUE, select antiques & memorabilia A-L, select beer can collectibles
Message Board:
GO ANTIQUE, select antiques & memorabilia A-L, select breweriana

Calculators & Computing Machines

World Wide Web
Antiques of Science and Technology
http://northshore.shore.net/~jim/welcome.html
Buy/Sell/Trade

Calculating Machines
http://www.webcom.com/calc/main.html
General Information, Links, Pictures

Collecting Calculators
http://www.geocities.com/SiliconValley/park/7227/
General Information, Buy/Sell/Trade, Links, Pictures

The Computer Specialist
http://www.tcomspec.com/index.htm
Buy/Sell/Trade

Historical Computer Society
http://www.cyberstreet.com/hcs/hcs.htm
General Information, Buy/Sell/Trade, Links

The Museum of HP Calculators
http://www.teleport.com/~dgh/hpmuseum.html
General Information, Buy/Sell/Trade, Links, Pictures, FAQs

The Slide Rule Home Page
http://photobooks.atdc.gatech.edu/~slipstick/slipstik.html
General Information, Links, Pictures, FAQs

The Typewriter Connection
http://home.earthlink.net/free/dcrehr/webdocs/collecting.html
General Information, Links, Pictures

Related Club/Association/Organization Sites

The Association for History and Computing
http://grid.let.rug.nl/ahc/welcome.html

The Calculator Collectors' Club
http://www.bath.ac.uk/~masres/calcs.html

The International Association of Calculator Collectors
http://www.bath.ac.uk/~masres/calcs.html

Carousel Art

World Wide Web

Carousel Classifieds
http://www.carousels.com/
General Information, Buy/Sell/Trade, Links, Pictures, Auction

America Online

Message Board:
GO ANTIQUE, select antiques & memorabilia A-L, select carnival & circus

Clocks, Watches, & Timepieces

World Wide Web

About Time
http://ourworld.compuserve.com/homepages/abouttime/
Buy/Sell/Trade, Pictures

Aldon Timeworks Inc.
http://ourworld.compuserve.com/homepages/Aldon_Timeworks_Inc/homepage.ht
General Information, Buy/Sell/Trade, Links

America Watch U.S.
http://208.128.40.80:80/eliwatch/
Buy/Sell/Trade, Pictures

Anglo American Antiques Ltd.
http://www.swcp.com/~antique
General Information, Buy/Sell/Trade, Links, Pictures

Antique Watches.com
http://www.antiquewatches.com/
General Information, Buy/Sell/Trade, Pictures

Antique-World
http://www.antique-world.com/
General Information, Buy/Sell/Trade, Pictures

Charles Edwin Inc.
http://www.charles-edwin.com/
General Information, Buy/Sell/Trade, Pictures

The Clock Doc
http://www.netwide.net/users/clockdoc/home.htm
General Information, Buy/Sell/Trade, Links

Debby's Emporium
http://rampages.onramp.net/~debbyemp/
Buy/Sell/Trade

Finer Times Vintage Wrist Watches
http://www.finertimes.com/
Buy/Sell/Trade, Pictures

Gordon S. Converse & Co. Gret Antique Clocks
http://www.pond.com/~gsc/
General Information, Buy/Sell/Trade, Pictures

Hallmark Antiques
http://www.consulweb.com/hallmark/hallmark_a.html
Buy/Sell/Trade, Links, Pictures

Harmening Haus
http://www.netins.net/showcase/hhaus/
Buy/Sell/Trade, Pictures

Horology - The Index
http://www.horology.com/horology/
General Information, Links

It's About Time
http://www.bearsystems.com/time/
General Information, Buy/Sell/Trade, Pictures

Joy & Mac's Vintage Pocketwatches Home Page
http://home.earthlink.net/~joymc/
Buy/Sell/Trade, Pictures

M.O.S.T Watch and Clock Co.
http://www.tritco.com/most/most1.html
General Information, Buy/Sell/Trade, Links, Pictures, Auction

MARK VIII Vintage Pocket and Wristwatches
http://ourworld.compuserve.com/homepages/markviii/
Buy/Sell/Trade, Pictures

Mike's Web Site
http://www.webcom.com/z4murray/
General Information, Links

Modesto Horology
http://www.modesto-horology.com/
Buy/Sell/Trade

Price-Less Ads
http://www.pricelessads.com/
General Information, Buy/Sell/Trade, Links, Pictures

Princeton Antiques
http://www.webcom.com/~antiques/shops/princeton/welcome.html
General Information, Buy/Sell/Trade, Pictures

Strother Jewelry
http://members.aol.com/jeweler2/index.htm
Buy/Sell/Trade, Pictures

Texas Time
http://www.io.com/~txtime/
Buy/Sell/Trade, Pictures

Time Again
http://www.wristwatches.com/
Buy/Sell/Trade, Pictures

time zone
http://www.timezone.com/
General Information, Buy/Sell/Trade, Links

watchnet
http://www.watchnet.com/
General Information, Buy/Sell/Trade, Links, Pictures

Wingate's Quality Watches
http://www.onramp.net/wingates/
Buy/Sell/Trade, Pictures

Wristwatches by Pompadour
http://www.watchnet.com/
Buy/Sell/Trade, Links

Related Club/Association/Organization Sites
American Watchmakers-Clockmakers Institute's Unofficial
http://www.webcom.com/z4murray/awi.shtml
National Association of Watch and Clock Collectors, Inc.
http://www.nawcc.org/

Newsgroup
alt.horology

America Online
Message Board:
GO ANTIQUE, select antiques & memorabilia A-L, select clocks & watches

CompuServe
GO ANTIQUES, select clocks & watches
GO COLLECTIBLES, select timepieces

Prodigy
Jump to COLLECTING 1 BB, select jewelry & watches

Coca-Cola

World Wide Web
Bobby "Have a Coke and a Smile" Liao
http://xenon.stanford.edu/~liao/home.html
General Information, Buy/Sell/Trade, Links
Candle Co. Antiques & Gifts
http://www.magic.mb.ca/~candleco/index.html
Buy/Sell/Trade, Pictures
The Coca-Cola Bay
http://www.wolfenet.com/~jdolan/coke.html
General Information, Buy/Sell/Trade, Links
Coca-Cola Classic Collector's Corner
http://members.aol.com/daclassic1/home1.htm
General Information, Buy/Sell/Trade, Links, Pictures
Coca-Cola Trading Post
http://www.cocacola.com/trade/
Buy/Sell/Trade, Pictures
Keith's Coca-Cola Bottle Clearing House
http://www.geocities.com/Heartland/2983/index.html
Buy/Sell/Trade, Links
P. & D. Collectibles
http://iaswww.com/pdgifts.html
General Information, Buy/Sell/Trade

Robbo's Collectors of Coca-Cola Memorabilia
http://www.ctel.com.au/~robbo/index.htm
General Information, Buy/Sell/Trade, Links, Pictures

Russ Zinck's Coca-Cola page
http://www.getnet.com/~playboy/coke/
General Information, Buy/Sell/Trade, Links

Steve Fox Coke Bottles
http://www.geocities.com/WallStreet/3609/
Buy/Sell/Trade, Links

Steve's Coca-Cola Collection and Mini-Museum
http://www.tiac.net/users/cckid/
Buy/Sell/Trade, Links, Pictures

The Virtual Coca-Cola Bottle Museum
http://www.dreamscape.com/griffin/VCCBM.html
General Information, Buy/Sell/Trade, Links, Pictures

Newsgroup

alt.food.cocacola

Prodigy

Jump to COLLECTING 2 BB, select Coke/Pepsi/bev

Coin Collecting/Numismatists

World Wide Web

Affordable Jewelry and Precious Metals
http://www.ajpm.com
General Information, Buy/Sell/Trade

All Australasian Collectables
http://www.ozemail.com.au/~quincol
Buy/Sell/Trade, Links, Pictures

All Goods Online xion and Catalog
http://gate.cruzio.com/~ganesh/
General Information, Buy/Sell/Trade, Links, Auction

B&M Coin Company
http://www.csmonline.com/BandM
General Informatio

The Coin Collector's Home Page
http://emporium.turnpike.net/M/mikec/index.htm
Buy/Sell/Trade, Links, Auction

Coin Universe
http://www.coin-universe.com/sites/coinvlib.html
General Information, Buy/Sell/Trade, Links, Auction

Collectors Den
http://www.collectorsden.com/
Buy/Sell/Trade

E Pluribus Unum
http://www.cyberenet.net/~ratboy/Coins/
General Information, Buy/Sell/Trade, Links

Eagle Eye Rare Coins
http://web.coin-universe.com/eagle_eye/
General Information, Buy/Sell/Trade, Pictures, Price Guide

The Fair Market Coin Pricer
http://www.rarity.com/
Links, Price Guide

Heritage Rare Coin Galleries
http://www.csmonline.com/heritage
General Information, Buy/Sell/Trade

Mt. Vernon Coin Company
http://www.csmonline.com/mtvernon
General Information, Buy/Sell/Trade

National Coin Company
http://www.csmonline.com/nationalcoin
General Information

National Gold Exchange, Inc.
http://www.csmonline.com/coinworld/covers/nge.html
General Information, Buy/Sell/Trade

Numismatica
http://www.limunltd.com/numismatica/
General Information, Links, FAQs, Price Guide

Numismatists Online
http://www.numismatists.com
General Information, Buy/Sell/Trade, Auction

Professional Numismatist Guild, Inc.
http://www.csmonline.com/png
General Information

RCI
http://www.csmonline.com/rci
General Information

Teletrade
http://www.teletrade.com/teletrade/
Buy/Sell/Trade, Pictures, Auction

Western Reserve Numismatics
http://www.rarity.com/wrn/
Buy/Sell/Trade, Links

Related Publication Sites

Bank Note Reporter
http://www.krause.com/collectibles/html/br.html

Coin Demon's Newsletter
http://www.malakoff.com/coindemon.htm
Coin Prices
http://www.krause.com/collectibles/html/cp.html
Coin World
http://www.csmonline.com/coinworld/
Coins Magazine
http://www.krause.com/collectibles/html/cm.html
Numismatic News
http://www.krause.com/collectibles/html/nn.html
Trader's Horn
http://www.InstantWeb.com/t/thorn/home.htm
World Coin News
http://www.krause.com/collectibles/html/wc.html

Related Club/Association/Organization Site

The American Numismatic Association
http://www.money.org/

Newsgroup

rec.collecting.coins

America Online

Weekly Chat Session: Tuesdays, 10-11 p.m. ET
GO COLLECTORS, select Chat Rooms, select Collectors Conference Room
Coins area:
GO COLLECTORS select coin & currency

CompuServe

GO COLLECTIBLES, select coins/currency/ANA

Prodigy

Jump to COLLECTING 1 BB, select coins & currency

Coin-Op Machines

World Wide Web

Antique & Home Use Slot Machines
http://www.vegas.com/gaming/hardware/sltcoll2.html
Buy/Sell/Trade, Pictures
B-Bop Jukeboxes & Gameroom Goodies
http://pmadt.com/bebop/default.htm
General Information, Buy/Sell/Trade

GameRoomAntiques
http://www.GameRoomAntiques.com/
General Information, Buy/Sell/Trade, Links

PicturesNMALL
http://www.pinmall.com/index.html
General Information, Buy/Sell/Trade

Rick's Gameroom Collectibles
http://www-odp.tamu.edu/%7Eschulte/
General Information, Links, Pictures

America Online

Message Board:
GO ANTIQUE, select antiques & memorabilia A-L, select gumball/misc/small vending

Message Board:
GO ANTIQUE, select antiques & memorabilia A-L, select jukes/slots/pinball/vending

Comic Books

World Wide Web

1 if by Cards, 2 if by Comics
http://www.1ifbycards.com
Buy/Sell/Trade

BackCopies
http://www.guideline.com/
Buy/Sell/Trade

Casey's Collectibles Corner
http://www.csmonline.com/caseys/index.html
Buy/Sell/Trade

Chaos! Comics page
http://www.public.iastate.edu/~joeduff/chaos.html
General Information, Buy/Sell/Trade, Links, Pictures

Claw City
http://www.rpi.edu/~garram/
General Information, Links, Pictures, FAQs

Collectors Den
http://www.collectorsden.com/
Buy/Sell/Trade

Comic Book Web Ring
http://cavalcade-whimsey.com/comics/ring.html
Links

Comics from the Vortex
http://www-scf.usc.edu/~ceddy/comics/comics.htm
General Information, Buy/Sell/Trade, Links, Pictures

Comics n' Stuff
http://www.missouri.edu/~c617145/comix.html
General Information, Links, Pictures

The ComicWeb
http://www.comicweb.com/
General Information, Buy/Sell/Trade, Links

Dark Horse Comics
http://www.dhorse.com/index.html
General Information, Links

Dave's Comics
http://www.davescomics.com/
Buy/Sell/Trade

Disney comics
http://WWW.Update.UU.SE:80/~starback/disney-comics/
General Information, Links, Pictures

E-Z's Garage Sale
http://www.tir.com/~whatever/garage.html
Buy/Sell/Trade

Fanatech
http://www.fanatech.com/
Buy/Sell/Trade, Links

Fantasy Illustrated and Rocket Comics
http://www.jetcity.com/~rocket/tofc.htm
General Information, Buy/Sell/Trade, Pictures

General Informationna's home page
http://www.scar.utoronto.ca/~95bastal/
General Information, Links, Pictures

Goldmine Comics & Cards
http://www.grnet.com/goldmine/
Buy/Sell/Trade

Jon's Comics Cards and Collectibles
http://www.csmonline.com/jons
Buy/Sell/Trade

Kingdom Comics
http://marketpro.com/kingdomcomics/
Buy/Sell/Trade, Links

Literary Works
http://www.erinet.com/hegwood/works.html
General Information, Links, Pictures

Monster's Collectibles
http://taz.interpoint.net/~monster/
Buy/Sell/Trade, Pictures

The Mutant Pages
http://www.santarosa.edu/~sthoemke/x/x.html
General Information, Links

Neatstuff and Collectibles
http://www.tsrcom.com/neatstuff/
Buy/Sell/Trade, Links, Pictures
Nemesis
http://www.mtco.com/~nemesis/
Buy/Sell/Trade, Links
The Nonstop Collector's Forum
http://www.odyssee.net/~tom2/
General Information, Buy/Sell/Trade
Spawn
http://www.spawn.com/
General Information, Pictures
SpiffWare's Collectibles Marketplace
http://www.pagescape.com/fire/index.html
Buy/Sell/Trade, Auction

Related Publication Site
Comic Buyer's Guide
http://www.krause.com/collectibles/html/bg.html

America Online
Comics area:
GO COLLECTORS, select comic book collector's board

Prodigy
Jump to COMICS BB

Country Collectibles

World Wide Web
Attic Antiques Online
http://206.21.6.249:80/antiques/dealers/attic/
Buy/Sell/Trade, Pictures
Country Classic Antiques
http://www.rockies.net/~antique/
Buy/Sell/Trade, Pictures
Electric Fan Collectibles
http://www.tfs.net/~cbrandt/
General Information, Links, Pictures
Falcon-Wood
http://www.oldtools.com/
Buy/Sell/Trade, Links, Pictures
Glass Insulators
http://www.insulators.com/
General Information, Buy/Sell/Trade, Links, Pictures, FAQs

Related Publication Site
Fine Tool Journal
    http://www.wowpages.com/ftj/

Related Club/Association/Organization Sites
American Bell Association
    http://www.collectoronline.com/collect/club-ABA.html
American Fan Collectors Association
    http://www.tfs.net/~cbrandt/afca.htm
Mid-West Tool Collectors Association
    http://www.mwtca.org/
The National Association of Milk Bottle Collectors, Inc.
    http://www.collectoronline.com/collect/club-NAMBC-wp.html
National Insulator Association
    http://www.insulators.com/nia/index.htm
National Reamer Collectors Association
    http://www.his.com/~judy/reamer.html
The National Toothpick Holder Collectors Society
    http://www.collectoronline.com/collect/club-NTHCS.html
Pacific Northwest Tool Collectors
    http://www.tooltimer.com/PNTC.htm
Richmond Antique Tool Society
    http://206.225.8.253:80/oldtool/
Rocky Mountain Tool Collectors
    http://www.unm.edu/~tr1005/index.htm
Western New York Antique Tool Collectors Association
    http://137.238.51.88/WNYATCA/info.html

America Online
Nutcracker Collector's
Weekly Chat Session: second Friday of the month, 10-11 p.m. ET
    GO COLLECTORS, select Chat Rooms, select Collectors Conference Room
Message Board:
    GO ANTIQUE, select antiques & memorabilia A-L, select antique tins

Prodigy
    Jump to COLLECTING 2 BB, select tins

Depression Glass

World Wide Web
The Antiques Nook
    http://www.clark.net/pub/aaccspri/home.html
    Buy/Sell/Trade, Links

Apple Orchard Antiques
http://pages.prodigy.com/QAZX57A/index.htm
Buy/Sell/Trade

A Sweet Memory
http://netnow.micron.net/~lrtv/
Buy/Sell/Trade, Pictures

Attic Antiques Online
http://206.21.6.249:80/antiques/dealers/attic/
Buy/Sell/Trade, Pictures

Crow's Nest Antiques
http://www.antiquetexas.com/cna/crow.htm
Buy/Sell/Trade

Depression Delights
http://www.onr.com/user/pam/
Buy/Sell/Trade, Links

Depression Era Glass and China MegaShow
http://www.GlassShow.com/
General Information, Buy/Sell/Trade, Links

DG Shopper Online (Fee required)
http://www.teleport.com/~dgshoppr/
General Information, Buy/Sell/Trade

Hardtimes Glassware
http://www.nauticom.net/www/secbec/hardtimesglassware.htm
General Information, Buy/Sell/Trade

Karen Facer's Depression Glass Plus
http://www.jdweb.com/fantiques/
Buy/Sell/Trade

Renée Antiques
http://www.facets.net/facets/renee/
Buy/Sell/Trade, Links, Pictures

Rubina's Antiques etc.
http://www.polaristel.net/~antiques/
Buy/Sell/Trade, Pictures

The Rural Entrepreneur - The Antiques Store
http://members.aol.com/bjmccray/antiques.htm
Buy/Sell/Trade

Something Olde
http://netnow.micron.net/~rbirk/index.html
Buy/Sell/Trade, Links

Related Publication Site

DG Shopper Online
http://www.teleport.com/~dgshoppr/

Related Club/Association/Organization Site
National Depression Glass Association
http://www.teleport.com/~dgshoppr/ndga.html

Die Cast

World Wide Web
Action Racing Collectables
http://www.action-performance.com/arc/hmearc.htm
General Information, Buy/Sell/Trade, Pictures

Arne's Page: Mostly Matchboxes
http://www.rio.com/~arne/
Buy/Sell/Trade, Links, Pictures

Arthur Hu's Toy Collecting Page
http://www.halcyon.com/arthurhu/collect.htm
General Information, Buy/Sell/Trade, Links

Asheville DieCast
http://www.asheville-diecast.com/
Buy/Sell/Trade, Links

Collectible Toy Mart
http://www.winternet.com/~toymart/
Buy/Sell/Trade

Die Cast Toys
http://ourworld.compuserve.com:80/homepages/Ppro/diecastt.htm
General Information, Buy/Sell/Trade, Links, Pictures

Diecast Toys
http://www.csmonline.com/diecast
Buy/Sell/Trade

Evers Toy Store
http://marketplaza.com/evers/evers.html
Buy/Sell/Trade, Pictures

George's Matchbox Page
http://members.aol.com/gsagi/matchbox/index.html
General Information, Buy/Sell/Trade, Links, Auction

"Good Ol Toys"
http://www.winternet.com/~toymart/
Buy/Sell/Trade, Links, Pictures

"Just" Matchbox
http://members.aol.com/jstmtchbx/page1.html
General Information, Buy/Sell/Trade, Links

Hot Wheels & Diecast
http://www.ns.net/~rdavis/hw.htm
General Information, Buy/Sell/Trade, Links

Lost in Toys
http://ng.netgate.net/~lostntoys/
Buy/Sell/Trade, Pictures

'Matchbox'
http://www.stern.nyu.edu/~smalik/matchbox/mbmenu.html
General Information, Buy/Sell/Trade, Links, Pictures

Matchbox Action Central
http://www.matchboxtoys.com/
General Information, Links, Pictures

Mattel Hot Wheels
http://www.hotwheels.com/
General Information, Buy/Sell/Trade, Pictures

Mitchell's Diecast Collection
http://www.avana.net/pages/personal/mitchell/index.html
General Information, Buy/Sell/Trade, Links, Pictures

The Motor City Hot Wheel Connection
http://www2.netquest.com/~jackson/
General Information, Buy/Sell/Trade, Links

Neatstuff and Collectibles
http://www.tsrcom.com/neatstuff/
Buy/Sell/Trade, Links, Pictures

Racing Champions
http://www.racingchamps.com/
General Information, Pictures

ToyLink
http://www.toylink.com/
Buy/Sell/Trade, Links, Pictures

Tri 'S' Racing
http://www.cyberhighway.net/~nicks/
General Information, Buy/Sell/Trade, Links

The Wheeler Dealer
http://www.cris.com/~carpool/
General Information, Buy/Sell/Trade, Links

Related Publication Site

Die Cast Car & Track
http://www.trader.com/diecast/

Related Club/Association/Organization Sites

Die Cast Car Collectors Club
http://www.interaccess.com/diecast/

Diecast Toy Collectors Association
http://www.teleport.com/~toynutz/

Newsgroup
rec.toys.cars

America Online
Hot Wheels Collector's
Weekly Chat Session: first and fourth Fridays, 10-11 p.m. ET
GO COLLECTORS, select Chat Rooms, select Collectors Conference Room

Prodigy
Jump to COLLECTING 2 BB, select diecast & metal toys

Disneyana

World Wide Web
The Collectiblesnet
http://www.collectiblesnet.com/
General Information, Buy/Sell/Trade, Links
Disney
http://www.disney.com/
Buy/Sell/Trade, Pictures
Disney comics
http://WWW.Update.UU.SE:80/~starback/disney-comics/
General Information, Links
The Mouse Man's Web Page
http://mouseman.com/
General Information, Buy/Sell/Trade, Links
The Nonstop Collector's Forum
http://www.odyssee.net/~tom2/
General Information, Buy/Sell/Trade

CompuServe
GO DOLLS, select Disney collectibles

Dolls

World Wide Web
A Doll's House
http://www.scican.net/~sdecker/doll1.html
General Information, Links, Pictures
Cabbage Patch Central
http://www.easysource.com/toys/
General Information, Buy/Sell/Trade, Links, Pictures

CompuServe's Doll's Forum (On CompuServe: GO DOLLS)
http://directory.compuserve.com/Forums/DOLLS/abstract.htm
General Information

Doll City
http://www.geo-mall.com/rodbarto/dollcity/index.html
Buy/Sell/Trade

The Doll House Bookstore
http://www.csmonline.com/barbie/barbbook.html
Buy/Sell/Trade

The Doll Menagerie
http://www.dollmenagerie.com/
Buy/Sell/Trade, Pictures

The Doll Page
http://www.dollpage.com/
Buy/Sell/Trade, Links

Dolls, Gifts & More
http://www.wdsi.com/iaa/
General Information, Buy/Sell/Trade, Links, Pictures

DollWeb
http://www.cascade.net/dolls.html
General Information, Buy/Sell/Trade, Links, Pictures

Flossy's Dolls & Collectables
http://spiderwebb.com/flossy.htm
General Information, Buy/Sell/Trade, Links, Pictures

Homestead Gift Shop
http://www.homestead-gift-shop.com/
Buy/Sell/Trade

JBJ's
http://www.jbjs.com/
General Information, Buy/Sell/Trade, Pictures

Master Colllector Online
http://www.mastercollector.com/
General Information, Buy/Sell/Trade, Links, Pictures

My Dolly Dearest
http://1-web-bazaar-plaza.com/dearest/
Buy/Sell/Trade, Links

Nellie's Doll List
http://everink.com/ndl.html
Links

Queen of Hearts Collectibles
http://www.qohdolls.com/
Buy/Sell/Trade, Pictures

Roberta's
http://www.csmonline.com/robertas
Buy/Sell/Trade

Treasures & Dolls
   http://www.antiquedoll.com/
   Buy/Sell/Trade, Pictures

Related Publication Sites
Antique Doll World
   http://www.tias.com/mags/IC/AntiqueDollWorld/
Doll Reader
   http://www.cowles.com/magazines/mag/dol.html

Newsgroup
   rec.collecting.dolls

America Online
Weekly Chat Session: Mondays, 9-10 p.m. ET
   GO COLLECTORS, select Chat Rooms, select Collectors Conference Room
Message Board:
   GO ANTIQUE, select antiques & memorabilia A-L, select Kewpie collectibles
Figures & Dolls area:
   GO COLLECTORS, select dolls
Pangea Toy Network:
   GO TOY

CompuServe
   GO DOLLS
   GO ANTIQUES, select dolls & teddy bears

Prodigy
   Jump to COLLECTING 1 BB, select dolls

Ephemera

World Wide Web
100,000 Maps For Sale
   http://pages.prodigy.com/FL/maps4sale/maps4sale.html
   General Information, Buy/Sell/Trade, Links
Alien Antiques
   http://home.earthlink.net:80/~asimov/
   Buy/Sell/Trade, Links
Antebellum Covers
   http://www.antebellumcovers.com/
   General Information, Buy/Sell/Trade, Links

Antipodean Books, Maps & Prints
http://www.highlands.com/Business/Antipodean.html
General Information, Buy/Sell/Trade, Pictures

Antique Paper & Ephemera X-change
http://www.apex-ephemera.com/main.htm
Buy/Sell/Trade, Links

Antique Paper Collectibles
http://www2.eos.net/rcarso19/
Buy/Sell/Trade, Links, Pictures

Antiquities Historical Galleries Ltd.
http://www.rarities.com/
General Information, Buy/Sell/Trade, Pictures

Appalachian Arts
http://www.athens.net/~aarts/index.html
Buy/Sell/Trade

Archiving Early America
http://earlyamerica.com/index.html
General Information, Buy/Sell/Trade, Links, Pictures

Baldwin's Old Prints & Maps
http://www.visi.net/baldwins/
Buy/Sell/Trade, Links

Comic, Fantasy & Gaming Card Autograph Collectors Home Page
http://www.serve.com/ephemera/golees/artistautographs.html
General Information, Buy/Sell/Trade, Links, Pictures

The Drawing Room of Newport
http://www.drawrm.com/
Buy/Sell/Trade, Links, Pictures

Fantasy Illustrated and Rocket Comics
http://www.jetcity.com/~rocket/tofc.htm
General Information, Buy/Sell/Trade, Pictures

Frank Mulligan's National Geographic Clearinghouse
http://www.ubicom.com/projects/ngc/main.html
Buy/Sell/Trade

Hamilton's Book Store
http://www.goodbooks.com/
General Information, Buy/Sell/Trade

The Historian's Gallery
http://www.nr-net.com/history/
General Information, Buy/Sell/Trade, Links, Pictures

Historical Document Society
http://www.datacity.com/hds/
Buy/Sell/Trade, Links

History Buff's Home Page
http://www.serve.com/ephemera/historybuff.html
General Information, Links, FAQs, Price Guide

Mark'n'Liz Franklin
http://ourworld.compuserve.com/homepages/marknliz/
General Information, Buy/Sell/Trade, Links

The Old Bookroom
http://www.ozemail.com.au/~oldbook/
Buy/Sell/Trade

Palmetto Presence
http://www.csra.net/21mall/ppresence.htm
General Information, Buy/Sell/Trade

Paper Collectors Mall
http://www.historybuff.com/mall/
General Information, Buy/Sell/Trade, Links, Auction

Pfeiffer's
http://www.tias.com/stores/Pfeiffer/
General Information, Buy/Sell/Trade, Pictures

The Quill & Pen
http://www.cris.com/~Rbattles/
General Information, Buy/Sell/Trade

Second Story Books
http://www.paltech.com/secondstory/
General Information, Buy/Sell/Trade, Pictures

Spider's Web Antiques and Collectibles
http://www.nh.ultranet.com/~spider/
General Information, Buy/Sell/Trade, Links, Pictures

Timothy Hughes Rare & Early Newspapers
http://www.serve.com/ephemera/timothy/hughes.html
Buy/Sell/Trade

The Trade Card Place
http://www.tradecards.com/tcp/index.html
General Information, Buy/Sell/Trade, Links, Pictures

Twin Brooks
http://www.tiac.net/users/twinb/
General Information, Buy/Sell/Trade, Links

Vintage Collectibles
http://ourworld.compuserve.com/homepages/marknliz/
General Information, Buy/Sell/Trade, Links

Wal Moreau
http://www.moreau.com/
General Information, Buy/Sell/Trade, Links, Pictures

WHACO
http://www.erols.com/whaco1/
General Information, Buy/Sell/Trade, Pictures

Related Publication Sites

Paper Collectors' Marketplace
http://www.tias.com/mags/pcm/

Trader's Horn
http://www.InstantWeb.com/t/thorn/home.htm

Related Club/Association/Organization Site
Ephemera Society of America, Inc.
http://www.mcs.net/~riverow/ephemera.usa/

Newsgroups
rec.collecting.paper-money
rec.collecting.postal-history

America Online
Message Board:
GO ANTIQUE, select antiques & memorabilia A-L, select ephemera
Message Board:
GO ANTIQUE, select antiques & memorabilia A-L, select historic newspapers/media/documents

CompuServe
GO ANTIQUES, select ephemera

Prodigy
Jump to COLLECTING 1 BB, select paper collectibles

Fast Food Collectibles

World Wide Web
Arthur Hu's Toy Collecting Page
http://www.halcyon.com/arthurhu/collect.htm
General Information, Buy/Sell/Trade, Links
Collectors Den
http://www.collectorsden.com/
Buy/Sell/Trade
The Curtis Action Figure & Collectable Page
http://members.aol.com/caumaug427/page1.htm
Buy/Sell/Trade, Links
Debi's Fast Food Toys
http://www.cris.com/~Gabrielc/index.htm
General Information, Buy/Sell/Trade, Links, Pictures
Kid's Meal Premiums
http://www.ionet.net/~saylor/premiums.shtml
General Information, Buy/Sell/Trade, Links, FAQs
Melanie & Chloe's Disney Fast Food Toys Picture Library
http://www.hypersurf.com/~melchloe/index.html
General Information, Links, Pictures

Richard's Fast Food/Happy Meal Toy Page
http://www.getnet.com/~richarde/
General Information, Buy/Sell/Trade, Links

Sorrell Enterprises
http://ourworld.compuserve.com/homepages/trevor_sorrell/kidsmeal.htm
General Information, Buy/Sell/Trade, Links

The Unofficial Happy Meal Page
http://www.ionet.net/~saylor/happy.shtml
General Information, Buy/Sell/Trade, Links

Related Club/Association/Organization Site

The McDonald's Collector's Club Web Page
http://www.cris.com/~Gabrielc/McDclub2.htm

CompuServe

GO COLLECTIBLES, select fast food/ornaments

Prodigy

Jump to COLLECTING 2 BB, select fast food items

Fine Art & Antiquities

World Wide Web

19th Century America
http://www.bmark.com/19thc.antiques/
General Information, Buy/Sell/Trade, Pictures

Aboriginal Arts
http://www.colorado.net/aboarts/home.html
General Information, Buy/Sell/Trade, Pictures

Animation and Fine Art Galleries
http://animationandfineart.com/
General Information, Buy/Sell/Trade, Pictures, FAQs

Antiquities Historical Galleries Ltd.
http://www.rarities.com/
Buy/Sell/Trade, Pictures

Artasian
http://www.artasian.com/index.html
General Information, Buy/Sell/Trade, Links, Pictures

Collectors' Corner
http://www.artcom.com/
General Information, Pictures

Curiox Web Treasure
http://www.spies.com/curiox/main/
Buy/Sell/Trade, Links, Pictures

The Drawing Room of Newport
http://www.drawrm.com/
Buy/Sell/Trade, Links, Pictures

Malter Galleries
http://members.aol.com/rarearts/malter/gallery.html
General Information, Buy/Sell/Trade, Pictures

Medusa Antiquities
http://www.anawati.com/
Buy/Sell/Trade, Pictures

Sadigh Gallery of Ancient Arts
http://www.ipgroup.com/sadigh/
Buy/Sell/Trade, Pictures

Young Fine Arts Auctionions, Inc.
http://www.maine.com/yfa/
Buy/Sell/Trade, Pictures, Auction

Related Publication Site

The American Antiquities Journal
http://www.americanantiquities.com/journal.html

Related Club/Association/Organization Sites

The International Paperweight Society
http://www.armory.com/~larry/ips.html

Paperweight Collectors' Association
http://www.collectoronline.com/collect/paperweight/PCA.html

America Online

Message Board:
GO ANTIQUE, select antiques & memorabilia A-L, select antique art items

CompuServe

GO ANTIQUES, select Young Fine Arts

Prodigy

Jump to COLLECTING 1 BB, select art

Furniture

World Wide Web

19th Century America
http://www.bmark.com/19thc.antiques/
General Information, Buy/Sell/Trade, Pictures

Anglo American Antiques Ltd.
http://www.swcp.com/~antique
General Information, Buy/Sell/Trade, Links, Pictures

Chine Gallery
http://home.hkstar.com/~chine/home.html
Buy/Sell/Trade, Pictures

Cinnamon Hill Antiques
http://www.nashville.net/~awebber/cinnamon/
Buy/Sell/Trade, Pictures

The Drawing Room of Newport
http://www.drawrm.com/
Buy/Sell/Trade, Links, Pictures

Hallmark Antiques
http://www.consulweb.com/hallmark/hallmark_a.html
Buy/Sell/Trade, Links, Pictures

Isidora Wilke Inc.
http://www.infohaus.fv.com/access/by-seller/Magna_Cum_Laude_OnLine/isidorawil
Buy/Sell/Trade, Pictures

L'esprit
http://www.lesprit.com/
Buy/Sell/Trade, Pictures

Marianne's Antiques
http://www.sonic.net/antiques/
Buy/Sell/Trade, Pictures

R.H. Blackburn and Associates
http://www.overset.com/blackburn/
General Information, Buy/Sell/Trade, Pictures

Sally's Antiques, Collectables & Fine Olde Furniture
http://www.victoriaBC.com/guide/vicsh5.html
Buy/Sell/Trade

Southampton Antiques
http://www.souhantq.com/
Buy/Sell/Trade, Links, Pictures

Upscale Antiques from Upstate New York
http://www.frontiernet.net/~nickz/
General Information, Buy/Sell/Trade, Links, Pictures

America Online
Message Board:
GO ANTIQUE, select antiques & memorabilia A-L, select antique furniture/lighting dev.

CompuServe
GO ANTIQUES, select furniture

<u>Prodigy</u>
Jump to COLLECTING 1 BB, select furniture/household

Gambling Memorabilia

<u>World Wide Web</u>

Be-Bop Jukeboxes & Gameroom Goodies
http://pmadt.com/bebop/default.htm
General Information, Buy/Sell/Trade

Benn Dunnington's Casino Chip Collecting Page
http://www.ccad.uiowa.edu/~bdunning/chips/chips.html
General Information, Buy/Sell/Trade, Links, Pictures

Casino Chips, Links, & More
http://advertising-source.com/chips.htm
General Information, Buy/Sell/Trade, Links, Pictures

Casino Collectibles and Collectors
http://pages.prodigy.com/CasinoGaming/collect.htm
General Information, Links

Chequers
http://www.chequers.com/
General Information, Buy/Sell/Trade, Links

The Chip Connection
http://www.casino-chip.com/
General Information, Buy/Sell/Trade, Links, Pictures

Cyn's Casino & Gaming Web Guide
http://pages.prodigy.com/CasinoGaming/index.htm
General Information, Links

Gambler's World
http://www.olywa.net/blame/br05100.htm
Buy/Sell/Trade

Greg Susong's Casino Chip Collecting Page
http://ourworld.compuserve.com/homepages/chip_man/
General Information, Buy/Sell/Trade, Links

Quality Collectibles
http://www.wfcollect.com/chips/index.html
Buy/Sell/Trade

Robert's Casino Chip Collecting Page
http://pages.prodigy.com/chips/
General Information, Buy/Sell/Trade, Links, Pictures

Starchip Enterprises
http://ourworld.compuserve.com:80/homepages/starchip/
General Information, Buy/Sell/Trade, Links, Pictures

Steven Slemons's Casino Chip Collecting
http://www.netcom.com/~sssvs/index.html
General Information, Buy/Sell/Trade, Links

Theresa's Collectible Corner
http://shopper.lv.com/Scott/collect.html
General Information, Buy/Sell/Trade, Links
Top's Chip Emporium
http://www.montego.com/~top/index.html
Buy/Sell/Trade, Links
Vegas Collectible Casino Chips
http://www.globalmark.com/chips/
General Information, Buy/Sell/Trade, Pictures

Related Club/Association/Organization Site
Casino Chip & Gaming Token Collector Club
http://ourworld.compuserve.com/homepages/chip_man/clubpage.htm#ccgtcc

America Online
Message Board:
GO ANTIQUE, select antiques & memorabilia A-L, select gambling collectibles

CompuServe
GO COLLECTIBLES, select casino chips & tokens

Prodigy
Jump to COLLECTING 1 BB, select casino chips & items

G.I. Joe

World Wide Web
Ancient Idols Collectible Toys
http://www.ewtech.com/idols/starwar.htm
Buy/Sell/Trade, Pictures
CamPro International
http://www.best.com/~campro/
Buy/Sell/Trade, Links
Cotswold Collectibles
http://www.whidbey.net/~cotswold/
General Information, Buy/Sell/Trade, Pictures
HQ Online
http://www.bodnarchuk.com/headquarters_quarterly/magazine.html
General Information, Buy/Sell/Trade, Links
The Joe Depot
http://www.ewtech.com/gijoe/
General Information, Buy/Sell/Trade, Pictures
Neatstuff and Collectibles
http://www.tsrcom.com/neatstuff/
Buy/Sell/Trade, Links, Pictures

SpiffWare's Collectibles Marketplace
http://www.pagescape.com/fire/index.html
Buy/Sell/Trade, Auction

Two Guys Toys
http://ifb.com/two-guys/index.htm
Buy/Sell/Trade, Auction

Newsgroup
alt.toys.gi-joe

CompuServe
GO DOLLS, select GI Joe

Glassware

World Wide Web

19th Century America
http://www.bmark.com/19thc.antiques/
General Information, Buy/Sell/Trade, Pictures

A & A Dinnerware Locators
http://users.aol.com/Stadelbach/BauerPottery.htm
General Information, Buy/Sell/Trade

A Sweet Memory
http://netnow.micron.net/~lrtv/
Buy/Sell/Trade, Pictures

Across the Miles Antiques
http://www.usaor.net/cam/
General Information, Buy/Sell/Trade

The Antiques Nook
http://www.clark.net/pub/aaccspri/home.html
Buy/Sell/Trade, Links

Attic Antiques Online
http://206.21.6.249:80/antiques/dealers/attic/
Buy/Sell/Trade, Pictures

The Cedars Antiques
http://www.csmonline.com/cedars
Buy/Sell/Trade, Pictures

Collectibles "Inc"
http://pages.prodigy.com/GMVY23A/search.htm
Buy/Sell/Trade, Links

Crow's Nest Antiques
http://www.antiquetexas.com/cna/crow.htm
Buy/Sell/Trade

Depression Era Glass and China MegaShow
http://www.GlassShow.com/
General Information, Buy/Sell/Trade, Links

Eclectiques Carnival Glass & Collectibles
http://www.qadas.com/eclectiq/
General Information, Buy/Sell/Trade, Pictures

Elegant American Glass
http://www.wavefront.com/~eag/
General Information, Buy/Sell/Trade, Links

Hardtimes Glassware
http://www.nauticom.net/www/secbec/hardtimesglassware.htm
General Information, Buy/Sell/Trade

Iowa Antiques
http://pw2.netcom.com/~keefco/iowa.html
Buy/Sell/Trade

Kent Washburn Antiques
http://numedia.tddc.net/washburn/
General Information, Buy/Sell/Trade

L.H. Selman Ltd.
http://www.armory.com/~larry/lhs.html
General Information, Buy/Sell/Trade, Pictures

Renée Antiques
http://www.facets.net/facets/renee/
Buy/Sell/Trade, Links, Pictures

Rubina's Antiques etc.
http://www.polaristel.net/~antiques/
Buy/Sell/Trade, Pictures

Something Olde
http://netnow.micron.net/~rbirk/index.html
Buy/Sell/Trade, Links

Woodsland's Carnival Glass Page
http://204.233.167.250/woodsland/carnivalglass/
General Information, Buy/Sell/Trade, Links, Pictures, Auction

Related Club/Association/Organization Site

Phoenix & Consolidated Glass Collectors Club
http://www.collectoronline.com/collect/club-PCGCC-wp.html

America Online

Weekly Chat Session: Fridays, 9-10 p.m. ET
GO COLLECTORS, select Chat Rooms, select Collectors Conference Room

Glass & Crystal area:
GO COLLECTORS, select glass & crystal

CompuServe
GO ANTIQUES, select glass
GO COLLECTIBLES, select pottery/glass/china

Prodigy
Jump to COLLECTING 1 BB, select glass & crystal

Jewelry

World Wide Web

A Victorian Elegance
http://gator.net/~designs/
General Information, Buy/Sell/Trade, Links, Pictures

A Wink & A Smile
http://rampages.onramp.net/~wnksmile/
Buy/Sell/Trade, Links, Pictures

Adornment: Collectible Costume and New Art Jewelry
http://www.infinet.com/~dschneid/
Buy/Sell/Trade, Links, Pictures

The Bee's Knees
http://www.biddeford.com/~tbkkpt/
Buy/Sell/Trade

Collectible Costume Designer Jewelry
http://www.theplace2b.com/jewelry/
Buy/Sell/Trade, Links, Pictures

The Costume Jewelry Showcase
http://www.clever.net/graycat/jewelry/
Buy/Sell/Trade, Links, Pictures

Depression Delights
http://www.main.com/~dd/
Buy/Sell/Trade

Durwyn Smedley Antiques
http://www.smedley.com/smedley/
Buy/Sell/Trade, Links, Pictures

Edith Weber & Assoc. Antique Jewelry
http://www.ANTIQUE-JEWELRY.com/
General Information, Pictures, FAQs

GEMZ
http://members.aol.com/gemette/index.html
Buy/Sell/Trade, Pictures

The Glitter Box
http://www.crl.com/~pamfil/GLITTER.HTM
Buy/Sell/Trade, Links, Pictures

Globalarts.com
http://www.collectiblesnet.com/
Buy/Sell/Trade, Pictures

Good Time Collectibles
http://www.tias.com/stores/goodtime/
Buy/Sell/Trade, Pictures

Hillary's Antique Jewelry Store
http://www.pacificws.com/sea/jewelry.html
Buy/Sell/Trade, Links, Pictures

Jan's Vintage and Antique Jewelry
http://www.newgaia.com/jewelry/index.html
General Information, Buy/Sell/Trade, Links, Pictures

Liz Collectible Jewelry
http://www.lizjewel.com/
Buy/Sell/Trade, Pictures

Lovejoys Estate
http://www.nas.com/lovejoy/love.html
Buy/Sell/Trade, Pictures

Princeton Antiques
http://www.webcom.com/~antiques/shops/princeton/welcome.html
General Information, Buy/Sell/Trade, Pictures

Q-Tiques
http://www.tias.com/stores/qtiques/
Buy/Sell/Trade, Pictures

Reyne Hogan Antiques
http://www.tias.com/stores/RHA/
General Information, Buy/Sell/Trade

Something Olde
http://netnow.micron.net/~rbirk/index.html
Buy/Sell/Trade, Links

Tomorrow's Treasures
http://www.theplace2b.com/marcy/
Buy/Sell/Trade, Pictures

Valerie B. Gedziun Designer Costume Jewelry
http://www.valerie.oa.net/
General Information, Buy/Sell/Trade, Links, Pictures

Vintage & Collectible Costume Jewelry
http://www.theplace2b.com/jewelry/
Buy/Sell/Trade, Links, Pictures

Wit's End
http://www.tias.com/stores/witsend/
Buy/Sell/Trade, Pictures

America Online

Message Board:
GO ANTIQUE, select antiques & memorabilia A-L, select collectible jewelry

CompuServe
GO ANTIQUES, select jewelry

Prodigy
Jump to COLLECTING 1 BB, select jewelry & watches

Lamps & Lighting

World Wide Web
Aladdin Knights Home Page
http://www.aladdinknights.org/
General Information, Buy/Sell/Trade, Links, Pictures
Dennis Hearn Oil Lamp Collections
http://www.oillamp.com/
General Information, Buy/Sell/Trade, Links, Pictures
oldlamp.com
http://www.oldlamp.com/default.htm
General Information, Buy/Sell/Trade, Pictures
Shades of Antique
http://www.csmonline.com/shades
Buy/Sell/Trade

America Online
Message Board:
GO ANTIQUE, select antiques & memorabilia A-L, select antique furniture/lighting dev.

License Plates

World Wide Web
Allan Brown's HomePage
http://www.agate.net/~silvrfox/licplt.html
Buy/Sell/Trade, Links
Florida Only License Plates
http://www.vero.com/web/flplates.htm
General Information, Buy/Sell/Trade, Links, Pictures
The Great License Plate Trade Page
http://www.duke.edu/%7Edms10/plates.html
Buy/Sell/Trade
Joe's Homepage
http://attila.stevens-tech.edu/~jwasiele/
General Information, Links, Pictures

License Plate Collector's Home Page
http://users.aol.com/EdE/plates.htm
General Information, Links, Pictures

Michael Kustermann's License Plates Pages
http://danshiki.oit.gatech.edu/~iadt3mk/LP_HP.html
General Information, Buy/Sell/Trade, Links, Pictures

PL8S Magazine
http://users.aol.com/pl8seditor/queen-b.htm/
General Information, Buy/Sell/Trade, Links, FAQs

Platesmenistan
http://www.cdi.org/~friedman/plates/
Buy/Sell/Trade, Links, Pictures

Ralph's US License Plate Page
http://www.man.katowice.pl/~labe/LicensePlates/Ralph/index.html
General Information, Buy/Sell/Trade, Links, Pictures

Washington State License Plate Info Station
http://weber.u.washington.edu/~bbirt/index.htm
General Information, Buy/Sell/Trade, Pictures

Yellky
http://helios.cto.us.edu.pl/~labe/LicensePlates/index.html
General Information, Buy/Sell/Trade, Links, Pictures

Limited Edition

World Wide Web

All About Christmas
http://www.holidaytree.com/
General Information, Buy/Sell/Trade, Pictures

Allen's
http://www.csmonline.com/allens
General Information, Buy/Sell/Trade

Angela's Florist & Gifts
http://home.earthlink.net/~angelasfg/
Buy/Sell/Trade

Angel's Hallmark
http://www.xmission.com/~cwood/hallmark.html
General Information, Buy/Sell/Trade, Links

Angie's Cherished Teddies Web Page
http://farside.cc.misu.nodak.edu/students/mckibbea/test.html
Buy/Sell/Trade, Links

Artistic Expressions of Ohio
http://www.cisnet.com/artistic/
Buy/Sell/Trade, Pictures

Atkinson's Gift Shop
http://www.phishnet.com/atkinsons/index.htm
General Information, Buy/Sell/Trade

Bears & Bedtime Mfg. (1994) Inc.
http://www.bearsandbedtime.com/index.htm
General Information, Buy/Sell/Trade, Pictures

Beartique
http://www.internauts.ca/beartique/
General Information, Buy/Sell/Trade, Pictures

Bell Tower Square
http://www.1stresource.com/c/christma/default.htm
Buy/Sell/Trade

Bob's Dickens Village Collection
http://www.athenet.net/~day/
General Information, Buy/Sell/Trade, Pictures, Price Guide

The Boyds Collector Forum
http://www.uconect.net/~onesource/
General Information, Buy/Sell/Trade, Links, Pictures, Price Guide

Cape Fear Christmas House
http://www.noel.com/
General Information, Buy/Sell/Trade, Pictures

The Cherished Teddies Swap Shop
http://www.wco.com/~fozzie/
General Information, Buy/Sell/Trade, Links

The Christmas Loft
http://christmasloft.com/christmasloft/welcome.htm
General Information, Buy/Sell/Trade, Pictures

The Christmas Shoppe Online
http://www.instantech.com/xmas_shop/index.html
General Information, Buy/Sell/Trade, Links, Pictures

Christy's Christmas
http://www.shopchristys.com/
General Information, Buy/Sell/Trade, Links

Coca Cola's Netalogue - Collectibles
http://www.cocacola.com/trade/collect.html
General Information, Buy/Sell/Trade, Pictures

Colleccity
http://ourworld.compuserve.com/homepages/colleccity/
General Information, Links

Collectible News
http://www.talcott.com:80/CollectNET/
General Information, Buy/Sell/Trade, Links, Pictures

The Collectiblesnet
http://www.collectiblesnet.com/
General Information, Buy/Sell/Trade, Links

Collector's Cove
http://kato.theramp.net/collectorscove/index.htm
General Information, Buy/Sell/Trade

Corner Collections
http://www.cornercollections.com/
Buy/Sell/Trade, Pictures

Crystallia
http://www.catmanor.com/moonbeam/crystallia/
General Information, Buy/Sell/Trade

Dancing Horse Antiques
http://www.csmonline.com/dancinghorse
General Information, Buy/Sell/Trade

David Winter Cottages Homepage
http://www.cs.umbc.edu/~sletsc1/DWC/
General Information, Pictures

Dolls, Gifts & More
http://www.wdsi.com/iaa/
General Information, Buy/Sell/Trade, Links, Pictures

The Elbourne Family
http://pages.prodigy.com/elbourne/dept56.htm
General Information, Links, Pictures

Essex Cottage Collectibles
http://www.webdirect.ca/essex/
Buy/Sell/Trade, Pictures

Exo Company
http://www.csmonline.com/exo
Buy/Sell/Trade

Ferrel's Hallmark
http://www.goldcrown.com/
General Information, Links, Pictures, FAQs

G and L Christmas & Gift Barn
http://www.gandlchristmasbarn.com/
General Information, Buy/Sell/Trade, Pictures

The Golden Goose
http://www.bbsnet.com/golden/
Buy/Sell/Trade

House of Bears
http://www.ultranet.com/~egf/www/house_of_bears/bears.shtml
General Information, Buy/Sell/Trade, Pictures

JBJ's
http://www.jbjs.com/
General Information, Buy/Sell/Trade, Pictures

Kringle Kottage
http://www.prairieweb.com/kringle/kk__home.htm
Buy/Sell/Trade, Pictures

Kris Kringl
http://www.kkringl.com/
General Information, Buy/Sell/Trade, Pictures

Linda's Hallmark
http://www.lindashallmark.com/
Buy/Sell/Trade, Pictures

Little Elegance
http://www.little-elegance.com/index.htm
General Information, Buy/Sell/Trade, Pictures, Price Guide

Michele's home page
http://ic.net/~mherr/
Buy/Sell/Trade

Moments On-Line
http://www.exp-online.com/moments/index.htm
General Information, Buy/Sell/Trade, Pictures

My-collectibles.com
http://www.my-collectibles.com/index.html
Buy/Sell/Trade

Nick & Grace Papaseraphim
http://www.users.interport.net/~papase95/index.html
General Information, Links, FAQs

North Pole City Collectibles
http://www.northpolecity.com/
Buy/Sell/Trade, Pictures

The Ornament Shop
http://www.catalog.com/cgibin/var/ornament/index.htm
General Information, Buy/Sell/Trade, Links

Over's Country Gifts
http://www.soundcity.net/~sover/index.html
Buy/Sell/Trade

P. & D. Collectibles
http://iaswww.com/pdgifts.html
General Information, Buy/Sell/Trade

Payless Collectibles
http://www.auntie.com/steve/main.htm
Buy/Sell/Trade, Pictures

Precious Moments Collectible Treasures
http://www.wjztv.com/kristi/sell.htm
Buy/Sell/Trade

Precious Plates 'N Things
http://web.idirect.com/~precious/
Buy/Sell/Trade, Links, Pictures

Quiet Horizons
http://www.quiethorizons.com/
Buy/Sell/Trade

Rhodas Collectibles
http://www.csmonline.com/rhodas
Buy/Sell/Trade

Riverton Drug and Gift
http://home.utah-inter.net/riverton-drug/
Buy/Sell/Trade, Pictures

The Roadrunner Hallmark
http://members.aol.com/gchallmark/hmk/index.html
General Information, Buy/Sell/Trade, Pictures

Rosie Wells Enterprises
http://www.RosieWells.com/
General Information, Buy/Sell/Trade

Ross Ernst
http://www.csmonline.com/collectors
Buy/Sell/Trade

Second Chance Collectibles
http://www.cyberpark-mall.com:80/second-chance/
General Information, Buy/Sell/Trade, Links

Something Olde
http://netnow.micron.net/~rbirk/index.html
Buy/Sell/Trade, Links

St. Nicks
http://www.epol.com/st.nicks/stnicks.html
Buy/Sell/Trade, Pictures

The Teddies Trader
http://www.feist.com/~yales/index.html
General Information, Buy/Sell/Trade

Teri's Cherished Teddies Page
http://www2.awinc.com/users/tcoady/
General Information, Links, Pictures

The World Collector's Net
http://www.worldcollectorsnet.com/
General Information, Buy/Sell/Trade, Links

Xanadu Cards and Gifts
http://www.sbusiness.com/xanadu/
Buy/Sell/Trade, Pictures

Yale's
http://www.feist.com/~yales/index.html
Buy/Sell/Trade

YuleLog Ornament Collection DataBase
http://www.wspice.com/forest/yulelog.htm
General Information, Buy/Sell/Trade, Links

Related Publication Sites

Figurines and Collectibles
http://www.cowles.com/magazines/mag/fig.html

Ornament Trader Magazine
http://www.webcom.com/netex1/orntrader.html
Rosie Wells Enterprises
http://www.RosieWells.com/Magazines.html
The Village Chronicle
http://www.villagechronicle.com/

Newsgroup

rec.collecting.villages

America Online

Hallmark Collectors weekly chat session: third Fridays of the month, 10-11 p.m. ET
GO COLLECTORS, select Chat Rooms, select Collectors Conference Room
Dept. 56 area:
GO COLLECTING, select Dept 56 Collecting

CompuServe

GO COLLECTIBLES, select fast food/ornaments

Prodigy

Jump to COLLECTING 2 BB, select cottages lighthouse
Jump to COLLECTING 2 BB, select dept 56
Jump to COLLECTING 2 BB, select enesco
Jump to COLLECTING 2 BB, select figures/limited edition
Jump to COLLECTING 2 BB, select Hallmark
Jump to COLLECTING 2 BB, select Precious Moments
Jump to COLLECTING 2 BB, select Swarovski

Magazines (Collectible)

World Wide Web

Adventure House
http://members.gnn.com/intandem/adv_hse.htm
Buy/Sell/Trade
BackCopies - Adult Magazine Catalogue
http://www.guideline.com/adult/ad-mm.html
Buy/Sell/Trade
Frank Mulligan's National Geographic Clearinghouse
http://www.ubicom.com/projects/ngc/main.html
Buy/Sell/Trade
Neatstuff and Collectibles
http://www.tsrcom.com/neatstuff/
Buy/Sell/Trade, Links, Pictures

Robert Dick Sports Publications
http://www.prozent.com/bobmags/INDEX.HTM
Buy/Sell/Trade

Prodigy

Jump to COLLECTING 1 BB, select books & magazines

Metals

World Wide Web

Abbott's Arcade of Antiques
http://members.aol.com/dwabbott/antiques.htm
General Information, Buy/Sell/Trade, Pictures, Price Guide

Affordable Jewelry and Precious Metals
http://www.ajpm.com
General Information, Buy/Sell/Trade

Anglo American Antiques Ltd.
http://www.swcp.com/~antique
General Information, Buy/Sell/Trade, Links, Pictures

D. Bigda Antiques
http://bmark.com/bigda.antiques/
General Information, Buy/Sell/Trade, Pictures

The Drawing Room of Newport
http://www.drawrm.com/
Buy/Sell/Trade, Links, Pictures

Hamilton's Book Store
http://www.goodbooks.com/
General Information, Buy/Sell/Trade, Pictures

MidweSterling
http://www.kcnet.com/sterling/index.html
Buy/Sell/Trade

Mirror Lake Antiques
http://www.bricom.com/mirrorlake/
Buy/Sell/Trade

Remember When Antiques
http://www.steeltree.com/remwhen/
Buy/Sell/Trade

Schredds of Portobello
http://www.clearlight.com/~schredds/home.htm
Buy/Sell/Trade, Links, Pictures

Related Publication Site

Silver Magazine
http://www.silvermag.com/

America Online
Message Board:
GO ANTIQUE, select antiques & memorabilia M-Z, select antique pewter
Message Board:
GO ANTIQUE, select antiques & memorabilia M-Z, select items from metals
Message Board:
GO ANTIQUE, select antiques & memorabilia M-Z, select antique silver

CompuServe
GO ANTIQUES, select metals
GO ANTIQUES, select silver

Militaria

World Wide Web
Alaska Enfield Headquarters
http://www.ptialaska.net/~akenfhq/
General Information, Buy/Sell/Trade, Links
Antique and Collectable Firearms and Militaria Headquarters
http://www.ibrowse.com/~mwade/SMA.htm
General Information, Buy/Sell/Trade, Links
Antique Militaria and Collectibles Network
http://www.collectorsnet.com/index.html
General Information, Buy/Sell/Trade, Links
Barry'd Treasure
http://www.iglou.com/btreasure/
General Information, Buy/Sell/Trade, Links, Pictures
C. Clayton Thompson - Bookseller
http://members.aol.com/Greatbooks/index.html
General Information, Buy/Sell/Trade, Pictures
Civil War @ Charleston, SC
http://www.awod.com/gallery/probono/cwchas/
General Information, Links
The Civil War Mall
http://members.aol.com/civwarmall/index.html
Links
Foley's Militaria
http://www.csmonline.com/foleys
Buy/Sell/Trade
Grande Armee Militaria
http://www.safari.net/~gama/
General Information, Buy/Sell/Trade
The Historian's Gallery
http://www.nr-net.com/history/
General Information, Buy/Sell/Trade, Links, Pictures

Jerry's Military Collectibles
http://www.bunt.com/~mconrad/jerry.htm
General Information, Buy/Sell/Trade, Links

Manion's
http://www.manions.com/
General Information, Buy/Sell/Trade, Pictures

Militaria Collectors Platoon
http://www.infonet.ee/platoon/
Buy/Sell/Trade, Links, Pictures

militaria.com
http://www.militaria.com/
General Information, Links

Naval & Military Press
http://www.csmonline.com/navalpress
Buy/Sell/Trade

Palmetto Presence
http://www.csra.net/21mall/ppresence.htm
General Information, Buy/Sell/Trade, Links

Red CyberBaron International
http://www.redbaronent.com/red2.htm
General Information, Buy/Sell/Trade, Links, Pictures

Sunset Pond Collectibles
http://members.aol.com/sunsetpond/index.htm
Buy/Sell/Trade, Links, Pictures

Wittmann Antique Militaria
http://members.aol.com/twittm350/index.html
General Information, Buy/Sell/Trade

World War II Books Home Page
http://www.sonic.net/~bstone/ww2books/
Buy/Sell/Trade

Related Publication Site

Military Trader
http://www.csmonline.com/militarytrader/

America Online

Message Board:
GO ANTIQUE, select antiques & memorabilia M-Z, select militaria

CompuServe

GO NOSTALGIA, select wars & politics

Prodigy

Jump to COLLECTING 1 BB, select militaria/political

Motorcycles

World Wide Web

AMCA Yankee Clipper
http://www.westwater.com/freezone/amca/
General Information, Links, Pictures

Classic Car Source
http://www.classicar.com/home.htm
General Information, Buy/Sell/Trade, Links

Harley Davidson
http://www.harley-davidson.com/
General Information, Pictures

Motorcycle Online
http://www.motorcycle.com/
General Information, Buy/Sell/Trade, Pictures

Starklite Indian Motorcycles
http://www.starklite.com/default.htm
General Information, Buy/Sell/Trade, Pictures

Related Club/Association/Organization Site

Antique Motorcycle Club of America, Inc.
http://ww1.comteck.com/~amc/

Movie & TV Memorabilia

World Wide Web

20th Century Productions
http://www.primenet.com/~toyrific
General Information, Auction

3-D
http://www.arenapub.com/MCW/ADZ/3D/3-D.html
Buy/Sell/Trade

BackCopies
http://www.guideline.com/
Buy/Sell/Trade

The Big Picture
http://www.dnai.com/~dnt/bigpix.html
Buy/Sell/Trade, Pictures

Cinemagic
http://www.webdep.com/cinemagic/
Buy/Sell/Trade, Pictures

Hollywood Boulevard
http://www.csmonline.com/hollywood
Buy/Sell/Trade

Hollywood Toy & Poster Company
http://www.hollywoodposter.com./
Buy/Sell/Trade, Links, Pictures

How Sweet It Was
http://www.csmonline.com/fisher
Buy/Sell/Trade

The Internet Movie Database
http://us.imdb.com/
General Information, Buy/Sell/Trade, Links, FAQs

LeMay Movie Posters
http://www.csmonline.com/lemay
Buy/Sell/Trade

Memorabilia Mine
http://www.memomine.com/
Buy/Sell/Trade

Movie Collector's World
http://www.arenapub.com/mcw/
General Information, Links, FAQs

Movie Memories
http://www.moviememories.com/index.html
Buy/Sell/Trade, Pictures

The Nonstop Collector's Forum
http://www.odyssee.net/~tom2/
General Information, Buy/Sell/Trade

The Nostalgia Factory
http://www.nostalgia.com/
Buy/Sell/Trade, Links

The Rural Entrepreneur - The Antiques Store
http://members.aol.com/bjmccray/antiques.htm
Buy/Sell/Trade

Silver Screen, Inc.
http://www.mo.net/silver/
Buy/Sell/Trade

Star Struck International
http://www.goodnet.com/~photos/starintl.htm
Buy/Sell/Trade, Pictures

TV Collectibles Trading Post
http://www.ravenet.com/tvland/index_tvcollectibles.html
General Information, Buy/Sell/Trade

Related Publication Sites

Big Reel
http://www.csmonline.com/bigreel/

Movie Collector's World
http://www2.arenapub.com/mcw/

America Online
Message Board:
GO ANTIQUE, select antiques & memorabilia M-Z, select rare movie items

CompuServe
GO NOSTALGIA, select nostalgia film
GO NOSTALGIA, select nostalgia music

Prodigy
Jump to COLLECTING 2 BB, select rock & roll/TV items

Music

World Wide Web
Andy's Record Supplies
http://www.csmonline.com/andys
Buy/Sell/Trade
ArtRock Online
http://www.artrock.com/
Buy/Sell/Trade, Links, Pictures
Augie's 45 RPM Vinyl Record Sale
http://home.earthlink.net/~augustl/45_RPM_Sale.html
Buy/Sell/Trade
Banana Records
http://www.csmonline.com/spotlight/banana
Buy/Sell/Trade
Bob Iuliucci
http://www.csmonline.com/iuliucci
Buy/Sell/Trade
The Book Garden Gallery
http://www.eden.com/~bgg/
General Information, Buy/Sell/Trade
California Albums
http://home.earthlink.net/~calalbums/index.htm
Buy/Sell/Trade, Auction
C.D.I. Video
http://www.csmonline.com/spotlight/cdiaudio
Buy/Sell/Trade
Cool Culture Media
http://www.eden.com/~bgg/culture/culture.html
Buy/Sell/Trade
Danny's Records
http://www.csmonline.com/displays/dannys
Buy/Sell/Trade

Dustry Groove America
http://dustygroove.com/
Buy/Sell/Trade, Links

Fast Hits Music
http://home.aol.com/FastHits
Buy/Sell/Trade, Links

Flipside Records
http://www.csmonline.com/flipsiderecords
Buy/Sell/Trade

Friendly Dealer's Of The Web
http://users.aol.com/recordwiz/private/fdotw.htm
Links, FAQs

GEM Records
http://www.mixi.net/~garym/records.html
Buy/Sell/Trade

Global Electronic Music Marketplace (GEMM)
http://gemm.com/
Buy/Sell/Trade

Harris, Steven Mark
http://www.csmonline.com/spotlight/harris
Buy/Sell/Trade

Hein's Rare Collectibles
http://www.csmonline.com/heins
Buy/Sell/Trade

Hot Platters
http://www.oversight.com/HotPlatters.html
Buy/Sell/Trade, Auction

Hot Wacks
http://www.csmonline.com/hotwacks
Buy/Sell/Trade

Jasper's Records
http://www.csmonline.com/jaspers
Buy/Sell/Trade

M & L Records and Models
http://www.halcyon.com/mlrecmod/
Buy/Sell/Trade

MisterE. Mail
http://www.wolfenet.com/~mistere/
Buy/Sell/Trade

Movie Poster List
http://www.musicman.com/mp/mp.html
General Information, Buy/Sell/Trade, Pictures

Music Marketplace Bookstore
http://www.csmonline.com/rocknroll/rockmags.html
Buy/Sell/Trade

Neatstuff and Collectibles
http://www.tsrcom.com/neatstuff/
Buy/Sell/Trade, Links, Pictures

Needles Express
http://www.csmonline.com/spotlight/needles
Buy/Sell/Trade

Neurotic Records
http://www.neurotic-records.com/
Buy/Sell/Trade

Paul's House of Music Vinyl Records
http://www.HUB.ofthe.NET:80/houseofmusic/
General Information, Buy/Sell/Trade, Links, Pictures, FAQs

Per Madsen Design
http://www.csmonline.com/spotlight/madsen
Buy/Sell/Trade

The Record Finder
http://www.recordfinders.com/
General Information, Buy/Sell/Trade, Auction

Rock'n Sports
http://www.csmonline.com/rocknsports
Buy/Sell/Trade

Rocktoys!
http://members.aol.com/rocktoys/index.html
Buy/Sell/Trade, Links

Scott Neuman's Forever Vinyl
http://www.exit109.com/~sneuman/fv.htm
Buy/Sell/Trade, Links

Sound Exchange
http://www.soundexchange.com/
Buy/Sell/Trade, Pictures

T-C's Record Rack
http://www.inworks.net/comm/tomstoy.htm
Buy/Sell/Trade

Time Warp Music Time Machine
http://www.vintage.com/mall/record/
General Information, Buy/Sell/Trade, Links, Pictures, Auction

Tunnel Records
http://www.csmonline.com/tunnel
Buy/Sell/Trade

Vintagemine
http://www.csmonline.com/vintagemine
Buy/Sell/Trade

Vinyl News
http://users.aol.com/vinylnews/private/vnews.htm
General Information, Buy/Sell/Trade

WonderYears Records
http://www.csmonline.com/wonderyearsrecords
Buy/Sell/Trade

The Write Source
http://www.csmonline.com/writesource
Buy/Sell/Trade

Related Publication Sites
DISCoveries
http://www.csmonline.com/discoveries/

Goldmine
http://www.krause.com/goldmine/

Newsgroups
rec.collecting.8-track-tapes
rec.music.collecting.cd
rec.music.collecting.vinyl
rec.music.marketplace.cd
rec.music.marketplace.vinyl

America Online
Weekly Chat Session: Sundays, 10-11 p.m. ET
GO COLLECTORS, select Chat Rooms, select Collectors Conference Room

Message Board:
GO ANTIQUE, select antiques & memorabilia M-Z, select sheet music

Message Board:
GO ANTIQUE, select antiques & memorabilia M-Z, select phonographs/music boxes

Record/Tape/CD collecting area:
GO COLLECTORS, select record/tape/CD collecting

CompuServe
GO COLLECTIBLES, select music collectibles

Prodigy
Jump to COLLECTING 1 BB, select music/records
Jump to COLLECTING 2 BB, select rock & roll/TV items

Musical Instruments

World Wide Web
All About Pianos!
http://pages.prodigy.com/pianos/
General Information, Buy/Sell/Trade, Links, Pictures

Hubbard Harpsichords
http://www.hubbard.qds.com/
General Information, Links, Pictures

Mechantiques
http://www.mechantiques.com/
Buy/Sell/Trade, Links, Pictures

Orange Coast Piano
http://www.mediawhse.com/ocoast/ocoast.html
General Information, Buy/Sell/Trade, Pictures

Player Piano
http://www.ruralnet.net.au/~mwaters/
General Information, Links, Pictures, FAQs

Steinway & Sons
http://www.g2g.com/steinway/index.html
General Information

Virtuoso Vintage Guitars
http://www.vvg.com/webframe.html
General Information, Buy/Sell/Trade

Voltage Guitars
http://southpaw.com/voltage/index.html
Buy/Sell/Trade

America Online

Message Board:
GO ANTIQUE, select antiques & memorabilia M-Z, select musical instruments

Native American

World Wide Web

Dancing Horses
http://galaxymall.com/shops/dancing_horses.html
General Information, Buy/Sell/Trade, Pictures

Golden Cloud, Ltd
http://hmt.com/gallery/goldencloud/
Buy/Sell/Trade, Pictures, Auction

Migrations
http://www.migrations.com/
General Information, Buy/Sell/Trade, Pictures

One Eyed Jack's Trading Post
http://www.dolphinshirt.com/oneeye/
Buy/Sell/Trade, Pictures

Sunshine Studio
http://www.trail.com/sunshine/
General Information, Buy/Sell/Trade, Links

Turkey Mountain Indian Arts
http://www.turkey-mountain.com/
Buy/Sell/Trade, Pictures

Wal Moreau
http://www.moreau.com/
General Information, Buy/Sell/Trade, Pictures

America Online

Message Board:
GO ANTIQUE, select antiques & memorabilia M-Z, select American Indian collectibles

Message Board:
GO ANTIQUE, select antiques & memorabilia M-Z, select tribal objects

Nautical

World Wide Web

Appalachian Arts
http://www.athens.net/~aarts/index.html
Buy/Sell/Trade

Down Memory Lane
http://www.shipsahoy.com/home.htm
Buy/Sell/Trade

Jonesport Nautical Art & Antiques
http://www.tiac.net/users/aegir/
Buy/Sell/Trade, Pictures

Maidhof Bros. Ltd Shipware
http://www5.electriciti.com/nautical/
Buy/Sell/Trade, Links, Pictures, Auction

Related Publication Site

Nautical Brass Online
http://members.gnn.com/nbrass/ezine.htm

America Online

Message Board:
GO ANTIQUE, select antiques & memorabilia M-Z, select nautical theme items

Orientalia

World Wide Web

Asian Arts
http://webart.com/asianart/
General Information, Pictures

Birdhouse Enterprises
http://www.thebirdhouse.com/index.htm
Buy/Sell/Trade, Pictures

East & Beyond, Ltd.
http://members.aol.com/eandbeyond/index.html
Buy/Sell/Trade, Pictures

I.M. Chait Gallery and Auctionion Home Page
http://www.inna.net/imc/index.html#top
Buy/Sell/Trade, Links, Pictures, Auction

Orientique
http://www.hk.super.net/~joeyf/orientiq/orientiq.htm
General Information, Buy/Sell/Trade, Pictures

Robyn Buntin of Honolulu
http://sweb.srmc.com/buntin/
Buy/Sell/Trade, Pictures

Related Club/Association/Organization Site

The International Netsuke Society
http://www.netsuke.org/

America Online

Message Board:
GO ANTIQUE, select antiques & memorabilia M-Z, select Asian antiques

Message Board:
GO ANTIQUE, select antiques & memorabilia M-Z, select oriental antiques

CompuServe

GO ANTIQUES, select Asian arts/ceramics

Pens & Pencils

World Wide Web

Bill Acker's Fountain Pen Page
http://ourworld.compuserve.com/homepages/Bill_Acker/billpage.htm
General Information, Links, Pictures

Clague's Antiques and Collectibles
http://www.ncn.net/~mpcac/
Buy/Sell/Trade

Finer Times Vintage Pens
http://www.finertimes.com/
Buy/Sell/Trade, Pictures

The Floaty Pen Page
http://home.earthlink.net/~espatz/floaty/index.html
General Information, Buy/Sell/Trade, Links

Glenn's Pen Page
http://mindlink.net/glenn_marcus/mrcshp3.htm
General Information, Links

Hot Fountain Pens
http://www.oden.se/~boris/
General Information, Links, Pictures

Jim's Fountain Pen Site
http://ourworld.compuserve.com/homepages/Jim_Gaston/
General Information, Links, Pictures

Penthusiasm
http://www.uni-bonn.de/~uzs8pd/index.html
General Information, Buy/Sell/Trade, Links

Newsgroup

alt.collecting.pens-pencils

CompuServe

GO COLLECTIBLES, select pens & pencils

Personalities

World Wide Web

Adam West Fan Club Online
http://www.adamwest.com/
General Information, Buy/Sell/Trade, Pictures

Adventures of Superman
http://www.tripod.com/~davidschutz/index.html
General Information, Links

Amos n' Andy
http://www.geocities.com/Hollywood/2587/
General Information, Links, Pictures

Anne of Green Gables Mercantile
http://www.peinet.pe.ca/homepage/anne/homepage.html
General Information, Buy/Sell/Trade, Pictures

Betty Boop's Fan Page
http://www.macatawa.org/~gking2/
General Information, Links, Pictures

Elvisly Yours
http://www.elvisly-yours.com/
General Information, Buy/Sell/Trade, Links, Pictures, Auction

Felix the Cat
http://www.felixthecat.com/
General Information, Buy/Sell/Trade

Garfield's World
http://www.cs.bsu.edu/homepages/dhackney/paws/garfworld.html
General Information, Buy/Sell/Trade, Pictures

The He-Man and the Masters of the Universe Home Page
http://www.awod.com/gallery/rwav/ctyner/he-man.html
General Information, Buy/Sell/Trade, Links, Pictures

Laura's Warm Puppy Page
http://www.eden.com/~snoopy/
General Information, Links, Pictures

OldToyDude's Toybox
http://members.aol.com/oldtoydude/toybox.htm
Buy/Sell/Trade, Pictures

Pulp
http://members.aol.com/dotPulp/index.html
General Information, Links, Pictures, FAQs

Pulp Heroes From Pulp Magazines
http://www.cs.uku.fi/~vaisala/Pulp.html
General Information, Buy/Sell/Trade, Links, Pictures

Three Stooges Collectors Showcase
http://www.3-stooges.com/
General Information, Links, Pictures, FAQs

Warner Brothers Studio Store
http://www.studiostores.warnerbros.com/
Buy/Sell/Trade, Pictures

Related Club/Association/Organization Sites

The Official Betty Boop Fan Club
http://www.betty-boop.com/

Official Popeye Fanclub
http://www.midwest.net/orgs/ace1/

Peanut Pals
http://chelsea.ios.com/%7Eosman/ppals.html

Peanuts Collectors Club
http://www.dcn.davis.ca.us:80/~bang/peanuts/

America Online

Message Board:
GO ANTIQUE, select antiques & memorabilia M-Z, select historic/famous people memorabilia

Pez Dispensers

World Wide Web

Burlingame Museum of Pez Memorabilia
http://www.spectrumnet.com:80/pez/
General Information, Buy/Sell/Trade, Pictures

The Original World Famous PEZ Home Page
http://www.io.com/~pault/
General Information, Links, Pictures, FAQs

The PEZ Coop
http://www.PEZ-COOP.com/
General Information, Buy/Sell/Trade, Pictures

PEZ Dispensers
http://www.ewtech.com/pez-sj-glew/
Buy/Sell/Trade, Pictures

The PEZ Page
http://www.concentric.net/~towncoin/index_html/pez/pez.html
Buy/Sell/Trade

PEZ.org
http://www.pez.org/
General Information, Buy/Sell/Trade, Links, Pictures, FAQs, Price Guide

Planet PEZ
http://pez.uark.edu/
General Information, Links, Pictures

Newsgroup
alt.food.pez

Prodigy
Jump to COLLECTING 2 BB, select pez

Phonecards

World Wide Web

A&K Telecards
http://www.hooked.net/~akakiona/
Buy/Sell/Trade

Acme Telecards Inc.
http://ourworld.compuserve.com/homepages/Acme_Telecards/
Buy/Sell/Trade, Links, Pictures

ACMI
http://www.phonecard.com/
Buy/Sell/Trade, Pictures

All Australasian Collectables
http://www.ozemail.com.au/~quincol
Buy/Sell/Trade, Links, Pictures

Bailey's Autographed Sports Cards & Memorabilia
http://www.tc.umn.edu/nlhome/m598/bail0099/cards.html
Buy/Sell/Trade

The Card Mall
http://www.cardmall.com/
General Information, Buy/Sell/Trade, Links

Card Source-The Postcard Place
http://emporium.turnpike.net/~Culture/
General Information, Buy/Sell/Trade

Ivan's PhoneCard Homepages
http://www.basec.net/~iwhite/phncard.html
Buy/Sell/Trade, Links, Pictures

JAC Cards and Collectibles Home Page
http://www2.pcix.com/~jac/
Buy/Sell/Trade, Links, Pictures

The Mall of AmeriVox
http://pacific.telebyte.com/~kkettell/moav.html
Buy/Sell/Trade, Pictures

PCM Report On-Line
http://www.pcmreport.com/
General Information, Buy/Sell/Trade, Links, Pictures, Auction, Price Guide

Racing Cards West
http://clever.net/rcw/home.html
General Information, Buy/Sell/Trade, Links

RBI Collectables
http://ourworld.compuserve.com/homepages/RBI_Collectables/
Buy/Sell/Trade, Links

Sears Phone Card Department
http://ourworld.compuserve.com/homepages/phonecard/
General Information, Buy/Sell/Trade, Links

Related Publication Site

Moneycard Collector
http://www.csmonline.com/moneycard/

Newsgroup

rec.collecting.phonecards

CompuServe

GO COLLECTIBLES, select phone & moneycards

Photographica

World Wide Web

Antique & Classic Camera Web Site
http://home.aol.com/dcolucci
Buy/Sell/Trade, Links

The Brownie Camera Page
http://users.aol.com/Chuck02178/brownie.htm
General Information, Links, Pictures

Cedric L. Robinson-Books
http://www.clark.net:80/pub/rmharris/alldlrs/ne/06095ced.html
General Information, Buy/Sell/Trade, Pictures

Collecting Kodak Cameras
http://users.aol.com/camcollect/kodak.html
Buy/Sell/Trade, Links, Pictures

Hamilton's Book Store
http://www.goodbooks.com/
General Information, Buy/Sell/Trade

Media Specialties
http://www.mediaspec.com/GNET/mediaspecialties/
Buy/Sell/Trade, Pictures

Nancy's Antique Photos
http://www.chatlink.com/~paperdol/Welcome.html
Buy/Sell/Trade, Pictures

Online Camera Exchange
http://www.tfb.com/oce/oce.htm
Buy/Sell/Trade

Pacific Rim Camera
http://www.teleport.com/~pacrim/
General Information, Buy/Sell/Trade, Links

Photo Classics
http://www.goodnet.com/~photos/photo.htm
Buy/Sell/Trade, Pictures

Photocamera Collezioni
http://www.bhw.com/pcc/
Buy/Sell/Trade

Ritz Collectibles
http://www.ritzcam.com/
Buy/Sell/Trade

Selected Cameras
http://www1.shore.net/~hemenway/cameras.htm
Buy/Sell/Trade, Pictures

Related Club/Association/Organization Site

The Daguerreian Society
http://java.austinc.edu:80/dag/

America Online

Message Board:
GO ANTIQUE, select antiques & memorabilia M-Z, select camera collectibles

Message Board:
GO ANTIQUE, select antiques & memorabilia M-Z, select poster/photo/print/painting

Porcelain/Pottery

World Wide Web

19th Century America
http://www.bmark.com/19thc.antiques/
General Information, Buy/Sell/Trade, Pictures

A & A Dinnerware Locators
http://users.aol.com/Stadelbach/BauerPottery.htm
General Information, Buy/Sell/Trade

A Sweet Memory
http://netnow.micron.net/~lrtv/
Buy/Sell/Trade, Pictures

Abbott's Arcade of Antiques
http://members.aol.com/dwabbott/antiques.htm
General Information, Buy/Sell/Trade, Pictures

Allan & Company Antiques, Inc.
http://www.webinsights.com/allanantiques/
General Information, Buy/Sell/Trade, Pictures

American Pottery Exchange
http://home.earthlink.net/~bufe/APX/
General Information, Buy/Sell/Trade, Links

Anglo American Antiques Ltd.
http://www.swcp.com/~antique
General Information, Buy/Sell/Trade, Links, Pictures

Antique Antics
http://www.antiqueantics.com/
Buy/Sell/Trade, Pictures

Antiques Network
http://w3.one.net/~dfi/
Buy/Sell/Trade

The Bauer Pottery Page
http://users.aol.com/Stadelbach/BauerPottery.htm
General Information, Buy/Sell/Trade, Links, Pictures

Birdhouse Enterprises
http://www.thebirdhouse.com/index.htm
Buy/Sell/Trade, Pictures

Black Bear Antiques
http://www.together.net/~cbeaudin/
Buy/Sell/Trade

British Faire
http://www.csmonline.com/britishfaire
Buy/Sell/Trade

Candle Co. Antiques & Gifts
http://www.magic.mb.ca/~candleco/index.html
Buy/Sell/Trade, Pictures

The Cedars Antiques
http://www.csmonline.com/cedars
Buy/Sell/Trade, Pictures

Collectibles "Inc"
http://pages.prodigy.com/GMVY23A/search.htm
Buy/Sell/Trade, Links

Collective Past
http://web2.airmail.net/antiques/
Buy/Sell/Trade, Pictures

Cookie Jars & Collectibles
http://pages.prodigy.com/barbcokc/jars.htm
General Information, Buy/Sell/Trade

The Drawing Room of Newport
http://www.drawrm.com/
Buy/Sell/Trade, Links, Pictures

Durwyn Smedley Antiques
http://www.smedley.com/smedley/
Buy/Sell/Trade, Links, Pictures

Essex Cottage Collectibles
http://www.webdirect.ca/essex/
Buy/Sell/Trade, Pictures

The Fiestaware Collectors Page
http://nexus.admin.umkc.edu/people/joe/home.html
General Information, Links, Pictures

Franciscan Earthenware Collection Page
http://adage.berkeley.edu/~amnon/Starburst/Starburst.html
General Information, Links, Pictures

Gordon Litherland
http://www.csmonline.com/litherland
General Information, Buy/Sell/Trade

Hall China Collecting
http://www.cjnetworks.com/~mkennedy/hallhome.html
General Information, Buy/Sell/Trade, Links

Hallmark Antiques
http://www.consulweb.com/hallmark/hallmark_a.html
Buy/Sell/Trade, Links, Pictures

J.R. Antiques & China Registry
http://www.islandnet.com/~cvcprod/jrantiq.html
General Information, Buy/Sell/Trade, Pictures

Jay's Fiesta and Antiques
http://www.flash.net/~mckinsey/INDEX.HTM
Buy/Sell/Trade, Links

Jim's Homepage
http://www.oswego.edu/~bcapelin/
Buy/Sell/Trade

Page Antiques, Fine Art & Collectibles
http://mindlink.bc.ca/Page_Antiques/page.htm
General Information, Buy/Sell/Trade, Pictures

Princeton Antiques
http://www.webcom.com/~antiques/shops/princeton/welcome.html
General Information, Buy/Sell/Trade, Pictures

Red Wing Town and Country by Eva Zeisel
http://www.mindspring.com/~dway/town.html
General Information, Buy/Sell/Trade, Pictures

Remember When Antiques
http://www.steeltree.com/remwhen/
Buy/Sell/Trade

Renée Antiques
http://www.facets.net/facets/renee/
Buy/Sell/Trade, Links, Pictures

Rubina's Antiques etc.
http://www.polaristel.net/~antiques/
Buy/Sell/Trade, Pictures

The Rural Entrepreneur - The Antiques Store
http://members.aol.com/bjmccray/antiques.htm
Buy/Sell/Trade

Russel Wright Web Page
http://www.feist.com/~thesuttons/rw/wright.html
General Information, Buy/Sell/Trade, Links, Pictures

Shirley Vickers
http://www.csmonline.com/vickers
General Information

Stangl Pottery Home Page
http://www.capecod.net/Wixon/stangl/stangl.htm
General Information, Buy/Sell/Trade, Links

Tea Leaf Ironstone China
http://ourworld.compuserve.com:80/homepages/da/
General Information, Buy/Sell/Trade, Links, Pictures

Treasure House Antiques
http://hosted-www.ftel.net/~hlclady/
General Information, Buy/Sell/Trade, Pictures

Warmark Antiques
http://www.doulton.com/warmark/index.htm
Buy/Sell/Trade, Links, Pictures

Watt On-Line
http://www.execpc.com/~wmhill/
General Information, Buy/Sell/Trade, Price Guide

Newsgroup

rec.crafts.pottery

America Online

Porcelain & China
Weekly Chat Session: Thursdays, except first Thursdays, 9-10 p.m. ET
GO COLLECTORS, select Chat Rooms, select Collectors Conference Room
Pottery
Weekly Chat Session: Thursdays, 10-11 p.m. ET
GO COLLECTORS, select Chat Rooms, select Collectors Conference Room
Porcelain & China collecting area:
GO COLLECTORS, select porcelain & china collecting
Pottery collecting area:
GO COLLECTORS, select pottery collecting

CompuServe

GO ANTIQUES, select pottery/porcelain
GO COLLECTIBLES, select pottery/glass/china

Prodigy

Jump to COLLECTING 1 BB, select cookie jars/salt & pepper/banks
Jump to COLLECTING 1 BB, select dinnerware/china
Jump to COLLECTING 1 BB, select pottery

Postcards

World Wide Web

California Cards
http://www.malakoff.com/postcards.htm
Links, Pictures
Card Source-The Postcard Place
http://emporium.turnpike.net/~Culture/
General Information, Buy/Sell/Trade, Pictures
Carl Seiler's Homepage
http://ourworld.compuserve.com/homepages/lcseiler/pcs.htm
General Information, Links, Pictures, FAQs
Jack Mount's Postcard Resources
http://dizzy.library.arizona.edu/users/mount/postcard.html
Links
Jim Mehrer's Postal History Page
http://home.revealed.net/mehrer/inx.html
General Information, Buy/Sell/Trade, Links, Auction

Kraze Ed's Postcard Page
http://www.web-pac.com/mall/kraze-ed/
General Information, Buy/Sell/Trade

Lars-Olov Stenborg's Postcard Home Page
http://www.algonet.se/~stenborg/pchome.html
General Information, Buy/Sell/Trade, Links, Pictures

Mark'n'Liz Franklin
http://ourworld.compuserve.com/homepages/marknliz/
General Information, Buy/Sell/Trade, Links

Modern Postcard Sales
http://www.csmonline.com/modernpostcard
Buy/Sell/Trade

The Pacific Attic Online
http://www.harbornet.com/postcard/
General Information, Buy/Sell/Trade, Links

Parker Barrington's Homepage
http://www.ced.tuns.ca/~parkerb/
Buy/Sell/Trade, Pictures

Pfeiffer's
http://www.tias.com/stores/Pfeiffer/
General Information, Buy/Sell/Trade

Playle's Postcard Auctionions
http://www.netins.net/showcase/postcard/
Buy/Sell/Trade, Links, Auction

The Postcard FAQ Page
http://www-students.unisg.ch/~mmarchon/postcard/faq/index.html
General Information, Links, FAQs

Postcards International
http://www.csmonline.com/postcardsint
Buy/Sell/Trade

Postcard Obsessed
http://www.suba.com/~noodles/postcard_obsessed/pcobsess.html
General Information, Links, Pictures

The Postcard Post
http://www.borg.com/~postcard/index.html
General Information, Buy/Sell/Trade, Links, Pictures, Auction

Roger Harvey's Postcard Page
http://pwp.starnetinc.com/roger/postcard.htm
General Information, Buy/Sell/Trade, Links, Pictures

Unique Estate Appraisals
http://www.europa.com/~bowers/
Buy/Sell/Trade, Links, Pictures

Vintage Collectibles
http://ourworld.compuserve.com/homepages/marknliz/
General Information, Buy/Sell/Trade, Links

Related Publication Site

Barr's Post Card News
   http://www.tias.com/mags/barr/

Postcard Collector
   http://www.csmonline.com/postcardcollector/

Newsgroup

   bit.listserv.postcard

Prodigy

   Jump to COLLECTING 1 BB, select postcards

Posters

World Wide Web

Arnold Movie Poster Company
   http://www.movieposters.com/
   Buy/Sell/Trade

BackCopies
   http://www.guideline.com/
   Buy/Sell/Trade

Chisholm Larsson Gallery
   http://www.chisholm-poster.com/
   Buy/Sell/Trade, Pictures

Class Act Movie Posters
   http://valuweb.com/valuweb/classact/
   Buy/Sell/Trade, Links, Pictures

CyberCinema
   http://www.cyber-cinema.com/
   Buy/Sell/Trade, Pictures

Hamilton's Book Store
   http://www.goodbooks.com/
   General Information, Buy/Sell/Trade, Pictures

Hollywood Toy & Poster Company
   http://www.hollywoodposter.com./
   Buy/Sell/Trade, Links, Pictures

How Sweet It Was
   http://www.csmonline.com/fisher
   Buy/Sell/Trade

JS Dietz Movie Posters
   http://www.io.com/~jsdietz/poster.html
   Buy/Sell/Trade, Pictures

LeMay Movie Posters
http://www.csmonline.com/lemay
Buy/Sell/Trade

Movie Poster Page
http://www.musicman.com/mp/posters.html
General Information, Buy/Sell/Trade, Pictures

Movie Poster Warehouse
http://www.movieposter.com/
General Information, Buy/Sell/Trade, Links, FAQs

Neatstuff and Collectibles
http://www.tsrcom.com/neatstuff/
Buy/Sell/Trade, Links, Pictures

Phyllis Givens Hollywood Collectibles
http://www.arenapub.com/MCW/ADZ/Givens.html
Buy/Sell/Trade

Rick's Movie Graphics and Posters
http://www.ricksmovie.com/
Buy/Sell/Trade

The Rural Entrepreneur - The Antiques Store
http://members.aol.com/bjmccray/antiques.htm
Buy/Sell/Trade

America Online

Message Board:
GO ANTIQUE, select antiques & memorabilia M-Z, select poster/photo/print/painting

Prints

World Wide Web

Allen's Creations Inc.
http://www.allenscreations.com/
General Information, Buy/Sell/Trade, Links

American Antique Prints
http://www.infinitiv.com/cwprints/
Buy/Sell/Trade, Pictures

Antipodean Books, Maps & Prints
http://www.highlands.com/Business/Antipodean.html
General Information, Buy/Sell/Trade, Pictures

Appalachian Arts
http://www.athens.net/~aarts/index.html
Buy/Sell/Trade, Pictures

Art & Old Print Restorations
http://www.oldprints.com/
Buy/Sell/Trade, Links, Pictures

Art Connections
http://www.erols.com/villej/alldlr/artconn/artconn.htm
General Information, Buy/Sell/Trade, Pictures

Baldwin's Old Prints & Maps
http://www.visi.net/baldwins/
Buy/Sell/Trade, Links

Horizon Books
http://www.io.org/~errol/
General Information, Buy/Sell/Trade, Links, Pictures

Jonesport Nautical Art & Antiques
http://www.tiac.net/users/aegir/
Buy/Sell/Trade, Pictures

The Philadelphia Print Shop, Ltd.
http://www.philaprintshop.com/
General Information, Buy/Sell/Trade, Pictures

Red Bow Antiques
http://www.csmonline.com/redbow
Buy/Sell/Trade

America Online

Message Board:
GO ANTIQUE, select antiques & memorabilia M-Z, select poster/photo/print/painting

CompuServe

GO ANTIQUES, select books & prints

Quilts

World Wide Web

American Quilts
http://www.AmericanQuilts.com/
Buy/Sell/Trade, Pictures

Carol Telfer Antiques
http://granite.cyg.net:80/~btelfer/
General Information, Buy/Sell/Trade, Links, Pictures

Hickory Hill Antique Quilts
http://quilt.com:80/HickoryHill
General Information, Buy/Sell/Trade, Links, Pictures

Log Cabin Antique Quilts
http://www.flash.net/~logcabin/
Buy/Sell/Trade, Pictures

One Thousand Antique Handmade Quilts Online
http://www.oldquilt.com/
General Information, Buy/Sell/Trade, Pictures

Quilts Unlimited On-Line
http://www.comet.net:80/quilts/
Buy/Sell/Trade, Pictures

Radios

World Wide Web

Antique radio and phonograph
http://home.navisoft.com/horn/ths2.htm
General Information, Buy/Sell/Trade, Links

Antique Radio Classified
http://www.antiqueradio.com/
General Information, Links, Pictures

The Antique Radio Collector
http://members.aol.com/wrldradio/index.htm
General Information, Buy/Sell/Trade

Antique Radio Page
http://members.aol.com/djadamson/arp.html
General Information, Buy/Sell/Trade, Pictures

Classic Radio Gallery
http://cpu.net/classicradio/
General Information, Links, Pictures

D'Antiques, Ltd.
http://www.dantiques.com/index.htm
Buy/Sell/Trade, Pictures

Marty Bunis Home Page
http://www.conknet.com/~m_bunis/
General Information, Buy/Sell/Trade

Phil's Old Radios
http://www.accessone.com/~philn
General Information, Links, Pictures, FAQs

Radio-O-Rama Antique Radio's
http://www.metronet.com/~lilthug/radio/radio.htm
Buy/Sell/Trade, Pictures

Radiomania
http://host.web12270.claimname.com/radiomania/
Buy/Sell/Trade, Pictures

Related Publication Site

The Antique Radio Collector
http://members.gnn.com/richmann1/wrldradio/index.htm

Newsgroup

rec.antiques.radio+phono

America Online

Message Board:
GO ANTIQUE, select antiques & memorabilia M-Z, select radios/telephones/telegraph

Prodigy
Jump to COLLECTING 1 BB, select phonographs/radio/TV

Railroadiana

World Wide Web

Classic Rail Cars
http://www.classicrail.com/index.html
General Information, Buy/Sell/Trade, Pictures

The Collector's Corner
http://www.notry.com/trains.htm
General Information, Buy/Sell/Trade, Links

Express Depot
http://www.coredcs.com/~express/
General Information, Buy/Sell/Trade, Links

Highlron Exchange
http://www.highiron.com/
Buy/Sell/Trade

P.D.R.'s Train Shop
http://www.direct.ca/adz/pdr/pdr.html
Buy/Sell/Trade

The Rail Philatelist
http://www.collectors-mall.com/trp/trp.htm
General Information, Buy/Sell/Trade, Links, Pictures

Signal Station 71
http://pw2.netcom.com/~vinscal/index.html
Buy/Sell/Trade, Links

America Online

Weekly Chat Session: Saturdays, 9-10 p.m. ET
GO COLLECTORS, select Chat Rooms, select Collectors Conference Room
Railroad/Railfanning board:
GO COLLECTORS, select railroad/railfanning board

Rugs & Carpets

World Wide Web

Ambient Rare and Antique Carpets
http://www.antico.com/
General Information, Buy/Sell/Trade, Links, Pictures

Carol Telfer Antiques
http://granite.cyg.net:80/~btelfer/
General Information, Buy/Sell/Trade, Links, Pictures

Chine Gallery
http://home.hkstar.com/~chine/home.html
Buy/Sell/Trade, Pictures

George Fine Kilims
http://www.azartnet.com/finekilims/index.htm
General Information, Buy/Sell/Trade, Pictures

Great Rugs!
http://great-rugs.com/
Buy/Sell/Trade, Pictures

Oriental Rugs at Hard Cider Farm
http://www.mint.net/antiques/oriental.rugs/oriental.html
Buy/Sell/Trade, Pictures

Skaff's Oriental Rugs
http://www.skaffrugs.com/index.html
General Information, Buy/Sell/Trade, Pictures

The Worldwide Rug Market
http://www.orientalrugs.com/
General Information, Buy/Sell/Trade, Pictures

Woven Treasures
http://www.woventreasures.com/
Buy/Sell/Trade, Pictures

Related Publication Site

Oriental Rug Review
http://www.rugreview.com/orr.htm

Scientific & Medical Instruments

World Wide Web

Barometer Fair
http://glimmer.com/barometer/
Buy/Sell/Trade

Charles Edwin Inc.
http://www.charles-edwin.com/
General Information, Buy/Sell/Trade, Pictures

The Gemmary
http://www.zweb.com/rcb/
Buy/Sell/Trade, Links, Pictures

Locke's
http://www.dircon.co.uk/lockes/index.html
General Information, Buy/Sell/Trade, FAQs

Media Specialties
http://www.mediaspec.com/GNET/mediaspecialties/
Buy/Sell/Trade, Pictures

Scientific and Medical Antiques
http://fammed.utmem.edu/sf/sci_ant.htm
General Information, Links

Scientific Medical & Mechanical Antiques
http://www.bestware.net/smma/index.htm
General Information, Buy/Sell/Trade, Links, Pictures

Related Club/Association/Organization Site

The Antique Telescope Society
http://www1.tecs.com/oldscope/

America Online

Message Board:
GO ANTIQUE, select antiques & memorabilia M-Z, select tools/scientific/medical instruments

CompuServe
GO ANTIQUES, select scientific/medical

Sewing & Related Items

World Wide Web

Buttons etc.
http://www.OnlineToday.Com/users/buttons/
Buy/Sell/Trade, Pictures

Jim's Sewing Page
http://www.concentric.net/~simanco/sewing.html
General Information, Links, Pictures

The Online Antique Sewing Machine Resource Page
http://www2.hawaii.edu/~claw/sew/
General Information, Links, Pictures

Patterns from the 20-60's
http://www.crocker.com/~lee/patterns.html
Buy/Sell/Trade, Pictures

Tangled Threads Antique Sewing Machine FAQs,
http://kbs.net/tt/faq/index.html
General Information, Pictures

Related Club/Association/Organization Site

International Sewing Machine Collectors' Society
http://www.ismacs.com.au/

America Online
Message Board:
GO ANTIQUE, select antiques & memorabilia M-Z, select buttons
Message Board:
GO ANTIQUE, select antiques & memorabilia M-Z, select sewing items

Prodigy
Jump to COLLECTING 1 BB, select sewing & textiles

Sporting Memorabilia

World Wide Web

All About Golf Collectibles
http://www.worldgolf.com/wglibrary/collector/main.html
General Information

Antique Fishing Tackle Exchange
http://www.webcom.com/tackle/nvmain.html
Buy/Sell/Trade, Links

The Classic Angler
http://www.gorp.com/bamboo.htm
General Information, Buy/Sell/Trade, Price Guide

Derby Glass page
http://www.derbyglass.com/
General Information, Buy/Sell/Trade, Links

Federal Duck Stamp Home Page
http://www.fws.gov/~r9dso/homedk.html
General Information, Links, Pictures

Joe's Old Lures
http://www.joeyates.com/
General Information, Buy/Sell/Trade, FAQs, Auction

Leo M. Kelly, Jr's. Golf Directory and Old Chicago Golf
http://www.oldgolf.com/oldgolf/wel.html
General Information, Buy/Sell/Trade, Links, Pictures

Lure Lore & Other Such Stuff
http://www.execpc.com/~tjacomet/my00001.html
General Information, Links, Pictures

Mark's Page
http://members.aol.com/markv500/index.html
Buy/Sell/Trade

Mike's Tackle Box
http://www.signmeup.com/scripts/signmeup/online/online/release/online.dl
General Information, Buy/Sell/Trade, Links

Old tennis items
http://webcom.com/tackle/tennis.html
General Information, Buy/Sell/Trade

Railbirds
  http://ai2a.net/~neymo/railbird.htm
  Buy/Sell/Trade

Sam's Fishing Page
  http://www.enter.net/~husselman/sam.html
  General Information, Buy/Sell/Trade, Pictures, FAQs

Related Publication Sites

Decoy Magazine
  http://www.dbqinc.com/decoy/

RPM
  http://www.csmonline.com/rpm/

Related Club/Association/Organization Sites

Golf Collectors Society
  http://www.aquinas-multimedia.com/golf/index.html

National Fishing Lure Collectors Club
  http://www.gorp.com/cl_angle/canecoun/nflcc.htm

Racing Collectables Club of America
  http://www.action-performance.com/rcca/hmercca.htm

Newsgroup

  rec.collecting.sport.misc

America Online

Message Board:
  GO ANTIQUE, select antiques & memorabilia M-Z, select Kentucky Derby collectibles

Message Board:
  GO ANTIQUE, select antiques & memorabilia M-Z, select hunting/fishing/flea market

CompuServe

  GO ANTIQUES, select hobbies & sport

Prodigy

  Jump to COLLECTING 1 BB, select sports memorabilia

Sports Cards & Memorabilia

World Wide Web

1 if by Cards, 2 if by Comics
  http://www.1ifbycards.com
  Buy/Sell/Trade

707 Trading Cards
http://www.csmonline.com/707
Buy/Sell/Trade

A & K Sports Collectibles
http://www.csmonline.com/aksports
Buy/Sell/Trade

Allstar Autographs!
http://www.sundaypaper.com/www/allstar.htm
Buy/Sell/Trade

American Sports Cards
http://www.e-universe.com/amsptcds/index.htm
Buy/Sell/Trade, Links, Auction

Antiquities International Online
http://www.goodnet.com/~photos/antqy.htm
General Information, Buy/Sell/Trade

Autographs On-Line
http://www.n-link.com/~autograph/
Buy/Sell/Trade

Beckett Online
http://www.beckett.com/
General Information, Buy/Sell/Trade, Links

Bill Henderson's Cards
http://www.azww.com/hendo/
General Information, Buy/Sell/Trade, Links

Boekhout's Collectibles Mall
http://www.azww.com/mall.shtml
Links, Auction

Burbank Coins & Sportscards
http://www.lainet.com/~bcs/
Buy/Sell/Trade

CamPro International
http://www.best.com/~campro/
Buy/Sell/Trade, Links

The Card Mall
http://www.cardmall.com/
Buy/Sell/Trade, Links

The Card Zone
http://www2.ari.net/cardzone/cz.html
General Information, Buy/Sell/Trade, Links, Auction

Casey's Collectibles Corner
http://www.csmonline.com/caseys/index.html
Buy/Sell/Trade

Cat's Cards and Collectibles
http://users.aol.com/bcdealer/private/homepage.htm
Buy/Sell/Trade, Links, Auction

Celebrity
http://www.csmonline.com/allstar
Buy/Sell/Trade

Dave's Vintage Baseball Cards
http://www.gfg.com/baseball/
General Information, Buy/Sell/Trade, Links

The Edge-Man Cards & Collectibles
http://www.edgeman.com/
Buy/Sell/Trade

Fleer Skybox International
http://www2.interpath.net/interweb/skybox/
General Information, Links, FAQs

K Gold Collectibles
http://www.csmonline.com/kgold
Buy/Sell/Trade

Jeff's Sports Cards Sale
http://www.auburn.edu/~engelja/sales.html
Buy/Sell/Trade, Links

John Skilton's Baseball Links,
http://members.tripod.com/~JBR500/joshpag.htm
Links

Josh's Sports Cards Shop
http://members.tripod.com/~JBR500/joshpag.htm
Buy/Sell/Trade, Links

koinz/kardz
http://www.getkardz.com/
Buy/Sell/Trade, Auction

Man of Steal
http://www.csmonline.com/manofsteal
Buy/Sell/Trade

Mini Mall Trading Cards
http://www.erols.com/jilee/mainpage.htm
Buy/Sell/Trade

Moody's Collectibles, Inc
http://www.csmonline.com/moodys
Buy/Sell/Trade

The Ninth Inning
http://www.csmonline.com/ninthinning
Buy/Sell/Trade

The Nonstop Collector's Forum
http://www.odyssee.net/~tom2/
General Information, Buy/Sell/Trade

Neil Hoppenworth's Cards
http://www.csmonline.com/hoppcards
Buy/Sell/Trade

Paladins
http://www.goodnet.com/~photos/paladins.htm
Buy/Sell/Trade

Peggy's Baseball Cards
http://www.erols.com/pegbbcds/index.htm
Buy/Sell/Trade, Links

Pinnacle
http://www.pinnacle-brands.com/index.html
General Information

Racing Cards West
http://clever.net/rcw/home.html
General Information, Buy/Sell/Trade, Links

Racket Sports Heritage
http://www.clark.net/pub/rackets/home.html
General Information, Pictures

Rainbow Card Company
http://www.wwcd.com/rainbow/
Buy/Sell/Trade

Rock'n Sports
http://www.csmonline.com/rocknsports
Buy/Sell/Trade

Rocky's Autographs & Memorabilia
http://www.goodnet.com/~photos/rocky.htm
Buy/Sell/Trade

Scottsdale Baseball Cards
http://www.scottsdalecards.com/
Buy/Sell/Trade, Links, Pictures

Sif Cards
http://www.csmonline.com/sifcards
Buy/Sell/Trade

Signatures - Sports Autographs & Memorabilia
http://www.sportsmem.com/
Buy/Sell/Trade

Sportsnut
http://planet-hawaii.com/sportsnut/memora.html
Buy/Sell/Trade

Teletrade
http://www.teletrade.com/teletrade/
Buy/Sell/Trade, Pictures, Auction

Texas Sportcard Company
http://www.csmonline.com/texas
Buy/Sell/Trade

Thrill of Victory
http://www.csmonline.com/thrillofvictory
Buy/Sell/Trade

Unique Distributors
http://www.csmonline.com/unique
Buy/Sell/Trade

Upper Deck Online
http://www.upperdeck.com/index.html
General Information

Vintage Baseball Cards
http://www.teleport.com/~gbrandt/baseball.htm/
Buy/Sell/Trade, Links

World-Wide Collectors Digest
http://www.wwcd.com/index.html
General Information, Buy/Sell/Trade, Auction, Price Guide

Related Publication Sites

Sports Cards
http://www.krause.com/sports/html/bc.html

Sports Collector's Digest
http://www.krause.com/sports/html/sd.html

Sports Map Magazine On-Line
http://www.cardmall.com/sportsmap/

Trader's Horn
http://www.InstantWeb.com/t/thorn/home.htm

Tuff Stuff
http://www.csmonline.com/tuffstuff/

Newsgroups

rec.collecting.cards.discuss
rec.collecting.sport.baseball
rec.collecting.sport.basketball
rec.collecting.sport.football
rec.collecting.sport.hockey
rec.collecting.sport.misc

America Online

Weekly Chat Session: Mondays, 10-11 p.m. ET
GO COLLECTORS, select Chat Rooms, select Collectors Conference Room

Sports cards area:
GO COLLECTING, select sports cards collecting

Message Board:
GO ANTIQUE, select antiques & memorabilia M-Z, select sports memorabilia

Prodigy

Jump to TRADING CARDS BB

Stamps

World Wide Web

Alan Anderson's Stamp Store
http://www.halcyon.com/alana/stamplist.html
General Information, Buy/Sell/Trade, Links, Pictures

All Australasian Collectables
http://www.ozemail.com.au/~quincol
Buy/Sell/Trade, Links, Pictures

AmeriCom Philatelic
http://www.fred.net/americom/
Buy/Sell/Trade, Links

Bick International
http://www.4free.com/bick/
Buy/Sell/Trade, Links, Pictures

Bill's Philatelic Bargains
http://louise.dlcwest.com/~bill.boomer/
Buy/Sell/Trade

The Blue Eagle's Nest
http://www.infi.net/~blueagle/
General Information, Buy/Sell/Trade, Links

Cappa
http://www.best.com/~mleon/cappa.html
Buy/Sell/Trade

Celmark Corp
http://www.aksi.net/celmark/
Buy/Sell/Trade

Century Stamps
http://www.century-stamps.com/
General Information, Buy/Sell/Trade, Pictures

Coughlin's Home Page
http://www.teleport.com/~coughlin/
General Information, Buy/Sell/Trade, Links, Pictures

DJ's Stamps
http://ourworld.compuserve.com/homepages/djsstamps/
Buy/Sell/Trade, Links, Pictures, Auction, Price Guide

Don Black Stamps & Postcards
http://www.donblack.com/
General Information, Buy/Sell/Trade

Don Mullins - Homepage
http://www.seanet.com/~dlm/index.html
Buy/Sell/Trade, Links

ebourse, The Stamp Collecting Marketplace
http://www.ebourse.com/
General Information, Buy/Sell/Trade, Links

Ed Anderson's
http://www.ecastamp.com/
Buy/Sell/Trade, Links, Pictures

FJC's Stamp Page
http://members.aol.com/fcapolongo/stamps/fjcstamp.html
General Information, Buy/Sell/Trade, Links, Pictures

Gregory K. Deeter's Online Stamp Shop
http://www.flex.net/~greg/stamps.htm
General Information, Buy/Sell/Trade, Links

Henry Gitner Philatelists, Inc.
http://www.hgitner.com/
Buy/Sell/Trade

Historical Document Society
http://www.datacity.com/hds/home.html
Buy/Sell/Trade

Ivy & Mader
http://www.cluster.com/ivymader/
Buy/Sell/Trade, Auction

J.E. Stewart Philatelics
http://ourworld.compuserve.com/homepages/JESP/
Buy/Sell/Trade, Links, Pictures

Jim's Stamp Page
http://web2.airmail.net/mccainjm/stamp.htm
General Information, Buy/Sell/Trade, Links, FAQs

Joseph R. Luft
http://www.execpc.com/~joeluft/index.html
Buy/Sell/Trade, Links

Kansas City Stamp Shop
http://www.tyrell.net/~ceipg/
Buy/Sell/Trade, Links, Auction

Philatelic Dealer's Group
http://www.millennianet.com/rev/pdg.htm
General Information, Buy/Sell/Trade, Links

The Philatelic Trading Post
http://www.clark.net/pub/stamps/
General Information, Buy/Sell/Trade

Philatelic.com
http://www.philatelic.com/
General Information, Buy/Sell/Trade, Links

Ronald C. Alfin
http://www.computerworks.net/alfin/
General Information, Buy/Sell/Trade

Seaside Book & Stamp
http://Fox.NSTN.Ca:80/~gtucker/
General Information, Buy/Sell/Trade, Links

Stamp Auctionion Central
http://www2.interpath.net/devcomp/auctions.htm
General Information, Links, Pictures

Stamp Universe
http://www.stampworld.com/
General Information, Buy/Sell/Trade, Links

Stamps Mall
http://www.webcom.com/~tuazon/stamps.html
General Information, Buy/Sell/Trade

Unique Estate Appraisals
http://www.europa.com/~bowers/
General Information, Buy/Sell/Trade, Links, Pictures

US Mints
http://www.forwardedge.com/usmints.html
Buy/Sell/Trade, Links, Pictures

Related Publication Sites

Linn's Stamp News
http://www.csmonline.com/linns

Stamp Collector
http://www.krause.com/collectibles/html/sc.html

Scott Stamp Monthly
http://www.csmonline.com/scott/monthly.html

Trader's Horn
http://www.InstantWeb.com/t/thorn/home.htm

Related Club/Association/Organization Sites

The American Philatelic Society
http://www.west.net/~stamps1/aps.html

The China Stamp Society, Inc.
http://www.azstarnet.com/~gersten/China.Stamp.Society.html

International Stamp Dealers' Network
http://www.yaxcorp.com/isdn/isdn.htm

National Stamp Dealers Association
http://ally.ios.com/~fortun49/nsda.html

Philatelic Dealer's Group
http://www.millennianet.com/rev/pdg.htm

The Society of Costa Rica Collectors
http://www.intersurf.com/~hrmena/

Newsgroup

rec.collecting.stamps

America Online
Weekly Chat Session: Tuesdays, 9-10 p.m. ET
GO COLLECTORS, select Chat Rooms, select Collectors Conference Room
Stamps area:
GO COLLECTORS, select stamp & letter collecting

CompuServe
GO COLLECTIBLES, select stamps & covers

Prodigy
Jump to COLLECTING 1 BB, select stamps

Starting Lineup

World Wide Web
3-Star Collectibles
http://www.dhinternet.com/~bob/
Buy/Sell/Trade, Links
Collectible Toy Mart
http://www.winternet.com/~toymart/
Buy/Sell/Trade
CR TOYS & Collectibles
http://www.cet.com/~crtoys/
Buy/Sell/Trade
Fokes Starting Lineup Page
http://pages.prodigy.com/MLPD19A/slus.htm
General Information, Buy/Sell/Trade, Links
Gordon's SLU Stop
http://home.cwnet.com/sluhunt/
General Information, Buy/Sell/Trade, Links, Price Guide
J.B.'s SLU Empire
http://www.geocities.com/Colosseum/2644/
General Information, Buy/Sell/Trade, Links, Pictures
The Ninth Inning
http://www.csmonline.com/ninthinning
Buy/Sell/Trade
The Starting Lineup Cyberspace Oasis
http://oeonline.com/~slu2/index.html
General Information, Buy/Sell/Trade, Links
The Starting Lineup Page
http://www2.startinglineup.com/startinglineup/
General Information, Links, Pictures

Related Publication Site
The Starting Lineup Advisory Magazine
http://www.netaxs.com/people/romwil/slam.html

Newsgroups
alt.collecting.sports-figures
rec.collecting.sport.baseball
rec.collecting.sport.basketball
rec.collecting.sport.football
rec.collecting.sport.hockey
rec.collecting.sport.misc

Prodigy
Jump to COLLECTING 2 BB, select starting lineup

Star Trek

World Wide Web
3-Star Collectibles
http://www.dhinternet.com/~bob/
Buy/Sell/Trade, Links
Action Figure Collectors Page
http://www.unc.edu/~lbrooks2/playmate.html
General Information, Buy/Sell/Trade, Links
Ancient Idols Collectible Toys
http://www.ewtech.com/idols/starwar.htm
Buy/Sell/Trade, Pictures
CR TOYS & Collectibles
http://www.cet.com/~crtoys/
Buy/Sell/Trade, Pictures
D & S Sci-fi Toy World
http://members.aol.com/dnsroberts/index.htm
Buy/Sell/Trade, Pictures
D.C. Collectibles
http://members.aol.com/ceschildt/debs.html
Buy/Sell/Trade
Final Frontiers
http://www.nashville.com/~final.frontiers/
General Information, Buy/Sell/Trade
Goldmine Comics & Cards
http://www.grnet.com/goldmine/
Buy/Sell/Trade
IKE Action Figures & Playsets
http://home.stlnet.com/~ike01/toyindex.html
Buy/Sell/Trade

SpiffWare's Collectibles Marketplace
http://www.pagescape.com/fire/index.html
Buy/Sell/Trade, Auction

Star Pieces
http://www.csmonline.com/starpieces
Buy/Sell/Trade

Star System Enterprises
http://www.starsystem.com/
Buy/Sell/Trade, Links

Trek Collector's Paradise
http://www.vhm.com/trek/
Buy/Sell/Trade, Links

Trek Shop
http://members.aol.com/trekshop/index.htm
General Information, Buy/Sell/Trade, Links, Pictures, Price Guide

America Online
Weekly Chat Session: first Wednesday, 10-11 p.m. ET
GO COLLECTORS, select Chat Rooms, select Collectors Conference Room

Star Wars

World Wide Web
3-Star Collectibles
http://www.dhinternet.com/~bob/
Buy/Sell/Trade, Links

Ancient Idols Collectible Toys
http://www.ewtech.com/idols/starwar.htm
Buy/Sell/Trade, Pictures

CR TOYS & Collectibles
http://www.cet.com/~crtoys/
Buy/Sell/Trade, Pictures

D & S Sci-fi Toy World
http://members.aol.com/dnsroberts/index.htm
Buy/Sell/Trade, Pictures

D.C. Collectibles
http://members.aol.com/ceschildt/debs.html
Buy/Sell/Trade

E-Z's Garage Sale
http://www.tir.com/~whatever/garage.html
Buy/Sell/Trade

Entertainment Earth
http://www.entertainmentearth.com/
General Information, Buy/Sell/Trade, Links, Pictures, FAQs

Goldmine Comics & Cards
http://www.grnet.com/goldmine/
Buy/Sell/Trade

Lost in Toys
http://ng.netgate.net/~lostntoys/
Buy/Sell/Trade, Pictures

Neatstuff and Collectibles
http://www.tsrcom.com/neatstuff/
Buy/Sell/Trade, Links, Pictures

SpiffWare's Collectibles Marketplace
http://www.pagescape.com/fire/index.html
Buy/Sell/Trade, Auction

Star Pieces
http://www.csmonline.com/starpieces
Buy/Sell/Trade

Star Wars Action Figure Web
http://5ss.simplenet.com/swafw/index.html
General Information, Links, Pictures, FAQs

The Star Wars Collector Circle
http://www.nni.com/~spanky/swcc1~1.htm
General Information, Buy/Sell/Trade, Links, Pictures

The Star Wars Collector Online
http://www.teleport.com/~dpip/swc/swc.about.html
General Information, Links

The Star Wars Collectors Archive
http://www.cs.washington.edu/homes/lopez/collectors.html
General Information, Links, Pictures, FAQs

Star Wars Mega Page
http://pages.prodigy.com/lg88/swhome.htm
General Information, Buy/Sell/Trade, Links, Pictures, Price Guide

Star Wars The Power of Collecting
http://members.aol.com/pizadahut/star_war_page.html
General Information, Buy/Sell/Trade, Pictures

Star Wars Toy Resource Page
http://pages.map.com/~amyshea/swtoys.html
General Information, Links, Pictures

The Ultimate Star Wars Links Page
http://w3.one.net/~dreid/starwars/main.html
Links

Related Publication Site

The Star Wars Collector
http://www.teleport.com/~dpip/swc/swc.about.html

<u>Newsgroups</u>
> rec.arts.sf.starwars.collecting
> rec.arts.starwars.collecting

<u>America Online</u>
Weekly Chat Session: first Wednesday, 10-11 p.m. ET
> GO COLLECTORS, select Chat Rooms, select Collectors Conference Room

Textiles

<u>World Wide Web</u>
Antiques from The Drawing Room of Newport and The Zsolna
> http://www.drawrm.com/
> *Buy/Sell/Trade, Pictures*

Asian Arts Exhibits
> http://www.webart.com/asianart/textiles/textile.html
> *General Information, Pictures*

Collective Past
> http://web2.airmail.net/antiques/
> *Buy/Sell/Trade, Pictures*

The Drawing Room of Newport
> http://www.drawrm.com/
> *Buy/Sell/Trade, Links, Pictures*

Reflections of the Past
> http://www.victoriana.com/antiques/
> *Buy/Sell/Trade, Pictures*

<u>Related Publication Site</u>
Rags
> http://www.mcn.org/R/RAGS/Default.html

<u>America Online</u>
Message Board:
> GO ANTIQUE, select antiques & memorabilia M-Z, select antique textiles

<u>Prodigy</u>
> Jump to COLLECTING 1 BB, select sewing & textiles

Tobacciana

<u>World Wide Web</u>
Andy's Zippo Lighter Page
> http://www.4thave.com/zippo.html
> *Buy/Sell/Trade, Pictures*

Antiques by Gallery 23
http://www.cyberconnect.com/gallery23/
Buy/Sell/Trade, Links, Pictures

Highlander Antique Mall
http://www.hilndr.com/
Buy/Sell/Trade, Links

The International Vintage Lighter Exchange
http://www.vintagelighters.com/
Buy/Sell/Trade, Pictures

Lighters Galore/Plus
http://www.electriciti.com/jerry/index.html
Buy/Sell/Trade, Pictures

Red Bow Antiques
http://www.csmonline.com/redbow
Buy/Sell/Trade

The Zippo Store
http://www.thezippostore.com/
Buy/Sell/Trade, Pictures

Related Club/Association/Organization Sites

The Rathkamp Matchcover Society
http://www2.psyber.com/~rmsed/

Tin Tag Collectors Club
http://www.collectoronline.com/collect/club-TTCC.html

America Online

Message Board:
GO ANTIQUE, select antiques & memorabilia M-Z, select lighters/smoking items

Message Board:
GO ANTIQUE, select antiques & memorabilia M-Z, select matchbooks/match safes

CompuServe

GO COLLECTIBLES, select The Smoke Shop

Tools

World Wide Web

City Ice Company
http://www.csmonline.com/city
Buy/Sell/Trade

Dukk Antiques
http://www.toolspot.com/toolpage/
Buy/Sell/Trade, Links

The Electronic Neanderthal
http://www.cs.cmu.edu/~alf/en/en.html
General Information, Links

Joe's Antique Tools
http://members.aol.com/ccrank9/index.html
Buy/Sell/Trade, Pictures

Jon Zimmers Antique Tools
http://www.teleport.com/%7Ejonz/
General Information, Buy/Sell/Trade, Links, Pictures

Old Tools Front Porch
http://www.pangea.com/~rock/oldtools/
General Information, Links

Tool Timer
http://www.tooltimer.com/index.html
General Information, Buy/Sell/Trade, Pictures

The ToolSlug
http://www.ovnet.com/~kgibbs/
Buy/Sell/Trade, Links, Pictures

Related Publication Site

The Padlock Collector
http://www.csmonline.com/padlock

Toys

World Wide Web

20th Century Productions
http://www.primenet.com/~toyrific
General Information, Auction

Action Point Collectibles
http://home.earthlink.net/~actpoint/
Buy/Sell/Trade

American Pie Collectibles
http://www.ewtech.com/americanpie/
Buy/Sell/Trade, Links

Bear Essentials
http://www.thegrid.net/bear/bear.htm
Buy/Sell/Trade, Links, Pictures

The Big Red Toybox
http://www.bigredtoybox.com/
General Information, Buy/Sell/Trade, Links, Pictures, Auction

Blueprinter
http://www.csmonline.com/blueprinter
Buy/Sell/Trade

Cabbage Patch Central
http://www.easysource.com/toys/
General Information, Buy/Sell/Trade, Links, Pictures

CamPro International
http://www.best.com/~campro/
Buy/Sell/Trade, Links

Cascade Models
http://www.aa.net/~cascade/
Buy/Sell/Trade, Links

Casey's Collectibles Corner
http://www.csmonline.com/caseys/index.html
Buy/Sell/Trade

Collectibles "Inc"
http://pages.prodigy.com/GMVY23A/search.htm
Buy/Sell/Trade, Links

The Collectiblesnet
http://www.collectiblesnet.com/
General Information, Buy/Sell/Trade, Links

Collectible Toy Mart
http://www.winternet.com/~toymart/
Buy/Sell/Trade

Collector Heaven
http://www.tiac.net/users/richz/
Buy/Sell/Trade, Links, Pictures

Collector Toy Network
http://www.sound.net/~stratton/
Buy/Sell/Trade, Links, Pictures

Cool Toy Shop
http://www.cooltoys.com/
Buy/Sell/Trade, Links

CR Toys & Collectibles
http://www.cet.com/~crtoys/
Buy/Sell/Trade, Pictures

D&K Toy Collectibles
http://www.csmonline.com/dktoy
Buy/Sell/Trade

Debby's Emporium
http://rampages.onramp.net/~debbyemp/
Buy/Sell/Trade

Die Cast Toys
http://ourworld.compuserve.com:80/homepages/Ppro/diecastt.htm
General Information, Buy/Sell/Trade, Links, Pictures

Diecast Toys
http://www.csmonline.com/diecast
Buy/Sell/Trade

Elmer's World
http://www.csmonline.com/elmers
Buy/Sell/Trade

Etch A Sketch
http://www.etch-a-sketch.com/welcome.html
General Information, Links

FAO Schwarz
http://faoschwarz.com/
Buy/Sell/Trade, Pictures

Funk and Junk
http://www.funkandjunk.com/collectibles.html
Buy/Sell/Trade, Pictures

Galoob Toys
http://www.galoob.com/
General Information, Pictures

Hake's Americana & Collectibles
http://www.hakes.com/
Buy/Sell/Trade

Hasbro Toys
http://www.hasbro.com/
General Information, Links, Pictures, FAQs

Heuser's Price Guide to Collectible Banks
http://www.concentric.net/~toybanks/index.htm
General Information, Buy/Sell/Trade, Links

Jon Bevans Collectibles
http://www.erols.com/jbevans/
Buy/Sell/Trade, Links

Land of Lunchboxes
http://www2.ari.net/home/
General Information, Pictures, Price Guide

The Lost in Space Collectors Page
http://lostinspace.buffnet.net/index.html
General Information, Buy/Sell/Trade, Links, Pictures, Price Guide

M & E Gizmos
http://pages.prodigy.com/JCQW47A/
Buy/Sell/Trade, Links

The Magical World of Fisher-Price
http://www2.best.com/~elusive/fisher_price/index.html
General Information, Buy/Sell/Trade, Links, Pictures, FAQs, Price Guide

Marble Collectors Corner
http://pages.prodigy.com/marbles/mcc.html
General Information, Buy/Sell/Trade, Links, Pictures, Auction

Master Colllector Online
http://www.mastercollector.com/
General Information, Buy/Sell/Trade, Links, Pictures

Monster's Collectibles
http://taz.interpoint.net/~monster/
Buy/Sell/Trade, Pictures

My Little Pony Trading Post
http://www.voicenet.com/~dsewalt/ponies.html
General Information, Buy/Sell/Trade

National Toy Connection
http://members.aol.com/NatlToyCon/ntc1.htm
Buy/Sell/Trade, Links, Pictures

Neatstuff and Collectibles
http://www.tsrcom.com/neatstuff/
Buy/Sell/Trade, Links, Pictures

OldToyDude's Toybox
http://members.aol.com/oldtoydude/toybox.htm
Buy/Sell/Trade

Pete's Toy Page
http://nweb.netaxis.com/~petebuilt/toys.html
General Information, Links

Playmates Toys
http://www.playmatestoys.com/toyshome.htm
General Information, Pictures

The Replica
http://www.csmonline.com/replica
General Information, Buy/Sell/Trade

Robots & Space Toys
http://www.mixweb.com/oneil/Spacetoys/
Buy/Sell/Trade, Links, Pictures

Santa Barbara Antique Toys
http://www.antiquetoys.com/
General Information, Buy/Sell/Trade, Links, Pictures

Showcase Collectibles
http://rampages.onramp.net/~showcase/
Buy/Sell/Trade, Links, Pictures

Spawn
http://www.spawn.com/
General Information, Pictures

Star Base One
http://www.starbase1.com/
Buy/Sell/Trade, Links, Pictures

Star Wars Mega Page
http://pages.prodigy.com/IG88/swhome.htm
General Information, Buy/Sell/Trade, Links, Pictures, Price Guide

Swap Shop
http://www.circa.com/viewmaster/home.html
General Information, Buy/Sell/Trade

Toy Scouts
http://www.csmonline.com/toyscouts
Buy/Sell/Trade

Toy Web
http://members.aol.com/toyweb/index.html
Buy/Sell/Trade

Toys of Yesterday
http://ally.ios.com/~dricha19/
Buy/Sell/Trade, Pictures

Twin Brooks
http://www.tiac.net/users/twinb/
General Information, Buy/Sell/Trade, Links

The View-Master Ultimate Reel List
http://ccwf.cc.utexas.edu/~number6/vm/
General Information, Pictures

Vintage Daze
http://members.aol.com/sacryed/vintage/frontpage.htm
Buy/Sell/Trade, Links

Virtual Flea Market
http://www.bright.net:80/~sschuler/flea.html
Buy/Sell/Trade

Related Publication Site

Collecting Toys
http://www.kalmbach.com/toys/collectingtoys.html

National Toy Connection
http://members.gnn.com/TNefos/ntc1.htm

Toy Market
http://www.cyberhighway.net/~nicks/

Toy Shop
http://www.krause.com/collectibles/html/ts.html

Toy Trader
http://www.csmonline.com/toytrader/

Wheel Goods Trader
http://www.wgtpub.com/

Related Club/Association/Organization Sites

American Game Collectors Association
http://www.usa.net/~rfinn/agca.htm

Newsgroups

rec.toys.misc
rec.toys.vintage

America Online
General Toys Discussion
Weekly Chat Session: Wednesdays, except the first Wednesday, 10-11 p.m. ET
GO COLLECTORS, select Chat Rooms, select Collectors Conference Room
Scale Modeling
Weekly Chat Session: Saturdays, 10-11 p.m. ET
GO COLLECTORS, select Chat Rooms, select Collectors Conference Room
Scale Modeling area:
GO COLLECTORS, select scale modeling collecting area
Toy Collecting areas:
GO COLLECTORS, select toy collecting A-L or M-Z
GO TOY

CompuServe
GO ANTIQUES, select toys

Prodigy
Jump to COLLECTING 1 BB, select toys (antique)
Jump to COLLECTING 2 BB, select toys (modern)

Trading Cards (Non-Sport)

World Wide Web
1 if by Cards, 2 if by Comics
http://www.1ifbycards.com
Buy/Sell/Trade
Audrey Simton
http://www.csmonline.com/simton
Buy/Sell/Trade
BackCopies
http://www.guideline.com/
Buy/Sell/Trade
Casey's Collectibles Corner
http://www.csmonline.com/caseys/index.html
Buy/Sell/Trade
Collectors Den
http://www.collectorsden.com/
Buy/Sell/Trade
CompuServe's Trading Cards Forum (On CompuServe: GO CARD
http://directory.compuserve.com/Forums/CARDS/abstract.htm
General Information

E-Z's Garage Sale
http://www.tir.com/~whatever/garage.html
Buy/Sell/Trade

The Edge-Man Cards & Collectibles
http://www.edgeman.com/
Buy/Sell/Trade

Final Frontiers
http://www.nashville.com/~final.frontiers/
Buy/Sell/Trade

Fleer Skybox International
http://www2.interpath.net/interweb/skybox/
General Information, Links, FAQs

HORROR FILM Trading Cards
http://sepnet.com:80/rcramer/hcards.htm
Buy/Sell/Trade

J & K Collectables
http://www.csmonline.com/jkcollectables
Buy/Sell/Trade

Jon's Comics Cards and Collectibles
http://www.csmonline.com/jons
Buy/Sell/Trade

Marchant Trading Cards
http://www.csmonline.com/marchant
Buy/Sell/Trade

Neatstuff and Collectibles
http://www.tsrcom.com/neatstuff/
Buy/Sell/Trade, Links, Pictures

Nonsport Card Collector's page
http://snapper.umd.edu/~rkohlbus/
General Information, Buy/Sell/Trade, Links, Pictures

Rainbow Card Company
http://www.wwcd.com/rainbow/
Buy/Sell/Trade

Sif Cards
http://www.csmonline.com/sifcards
Buy/Sell/Trade

Unique Distributors
http://www.csmonline.com/unique
Buy/Sell/Trade

Related Publication Site

Moneycard Collector
http://www.csmonline.com/moneycard

Newsgroups

rec.collecting.cards.discuss
rec.collecting.cards.non-sports

Trains

World Wide Web

Ace Hanses Hardware
http://iserve.bigweb.com/lioneltrain/
Buy/Sell/Trade

Aristo-Craft Trains Internet Depot
http://com.primenet.com/aristo/
General Information, Buy/Sell/Trade, Links, Pictures

Atlas Online
http://www.atlasrr.com/
General Information, Buy/Sell/Trade

The Attic Fanatic Model Train Store
http://www.hurricane.net/~trains/
Buy/Sell/Trade, Links

Bookbinder's "Trains Unlimited"
http://www.netpage1.com/bookbinderstrains/
Buy/Sell/Trade

Con-Cor
http://tucson.com/concor/
General Information, Links

Express Depot
http://www.coredcs.com/~express/
General Information, Buy/Sell/Trade, Links

Flyerville Station
http://www2.newriver.net/flyerville/
General Information, Buy/Sell/Trade, Links, Pictures, FAQs

H & R Trains
http://www.hrtrains.com/
General Information, Buy/Sell/Trade, Links

HighIron Exchange
http://www.highiron.com/
Buy/Sell/Trade

The Interchange Track
http://www.catch22.com/~spassmo/ggmrc/interchange.html
Links

King of the Road
http://www.execpc.com/~king/trains.html
Buy/Sell/Trade

Large Scale Online
http://www.largescale.com/
General Information, Buy/Sell/Trade

LGB of America
http://www.lgb.com
General information, Links, Pictures

Lionel Station
http://www.Lionel.com/
General Information, Links, Pictures

Mantua Collectibles
http://www.mantua.com/
General Information, Buy/Sell/Trade, Links

Marklin Trains
http://www.marklin.com/
General Information, Buy/Sell/Trade, Pictures

Marx Trains
http://www.trainexchange.com/marx.htm
General information, Links, Pictures

Mike's Train House (MTH) Electric Trains
http://www.mth-railking.com
General information, Links, Pictures

The Model Railroad Mall
http://www.walthers.com:80/
General Information, Buy/Sell/Trade

The RR Depot
http://www.virtual-village.com/rrdepot/index.html
General Information, Buy/Sell/Trade, Pictures

S Scale Model Railroading Homepage
http://www.connix.com/~crocon/sscale.html
General Information, Links

The Toy Train Exchange
http://www.trainexchange.com/
General Information, Buy/Sell/Trade, Links

Tractronics Incorporated
http://www.mcs.net/~weyand/
General Information, Links, FAQs

Train City
http://erie.net/~traincty/
General Information, Buy/Sell/Trade, Links

The Train Exchange
http://www.toytrain.com/~trains/welcome.html
Buy/Sell/Trade

Tried & True Trains
http://www.tttrains.com/
General Information, Buy/Sell/Trade, Links

Vintage Lionel Train Exchange
http://www.ghgcorp.com/lionel/lionel.html
General Information, Buy/Sell/Trade

Related Publication Site
Classic Toy Trains
http://www.kalmbach.com/ctt/toytrains.html

Related Club/Association/Organization Sites
Lionel Collectors Club of America
http://www.alliance.net/~lccane19
National Model Railroad Association
http://www.mcs.net/~weyand/nmra/nmrahome.html
Train Collectors Association
http://www.traincollectors.org/

Newsgroup
rec.models.railroad

Typewriters

World Wide Web
Antique Typewriter Collecting
http://members.aol.com/typebar/collectible/typewriter.htm
General Information, Pictures
The Classic Typewriter Page
http://xavier.xu.edu:8000/~polt/typewriters.html
General Information, Buy/Sell/Trade, Links, Pictures, FAQs
The Qwerty Connection
http://home.earthlink.net/free/dcrehr/webdocs/
General Information, Links, Pictures

Related Club/Association/Organization Site
The Early Typewriter Collectors Association
http://home.earthlink.net/free/dcrehr/webdocs/etc.html

Victorian Antiques

World Wide Web
19th Century America
http://www.bmark.com/19thc.antiques/
General Information, Buy/Sell/Trade, Pictures

Victorian Elegance
  http://gator.net/~designs/
  Buy/Sell/Trade, Links, Pictures
Victoriana
  http://www.victoriana.com/
  General Information, Links, Pictures

America Online
Message Board:
  GO ANTIQUE, select antiques & memorabilia M-Z, select victorian items

CompuServe
  GO NOSTALGIA, select Victoriana

Vintage Clothing

World Wide Web
A Victorian Elegance
  http://gator.net/~designs/
  General Information, Buy/Sell/Trade, Links, Pictures
American Vintage Classics
  http://www.angelfire.com/pages0/vintage/index.html
  Buy/Sell/Trade, Links
The Bee's Knees
  http://www.biddeford.com/~tbkkpt/
  Buy/Sell/Trade
The Cat's Pajamas
  http://www.Sunlink.net/~catspjs/
  Buy/Sell/Trade, Links, Pictures
Darrow Vintage Clothing
  http://www.darrowvintage.com/
  General Information, Pictures
Discover Yesterday
  http://www.quiknet.com/discover/
  Buy/Sell/Trade, Pictures
Harmening Haus
  http://www.netins.net/showcase/hhaus/
  Buy/Sell/Trade, Pictures
M.A. Blackburn
  http://www.csmonline.com/blackburn
  Buy/Sell/Trade
Reflections of the Past
  http://www.victoriana.com/antiques/
  Buy/Sell/Trade, Pictures

Rusty Zipper
http://www.rustyzipper.com/work/rzhelp.html
Buy/Sell/Trade, Links, Pictures

The Vintage Archives
http://www.cs.brown.edu/people/smh/vintage/vintage.html
General Information, Links

America Online

Message Board:
GO ANTIQUE, select antiques & memorabilia M-Z, select clothing & accessories

CompuServe

GO ANTIQUES, select clothing/accessories

Weapons

World Wide Web

Antique and Collectable Headquarters
http://www.ibrowse.com/~mwade/SMA.htm
General Information, Buy/Sell/Trade, Links

Antique Firearm Network
http://oldguns.com/
General Information, Buy/Sell/Trade, Links

Antique Militaria and Collectibles Network
http://www.collectorsnet.com/index.html
General Information, Buy/Sell/Trade, Links

Dixie Gun Works
http://oldguns.com/dixiegun/index.htm
Buy/Sell/Trade

Grande Armee Militaria
http://www.safari.net/~gama/
General Information, Buy/Sell/Trade

Irons in the Fire
http://www.redbaronent.com/
Buy/Sell/Trade, Links, Pictures

Old Town Station Dispatch
http://members.aol.com/OldTownSta/index.html
General Information, Buy/Sell/Trade

Peter Finer
http://www.peterfiner.com/index.html
General Information, Buy/Sell/Trade, Pictures

Sunset Pond Collectibles
http://members.aol.com/sunsetpond/index.htm
Buy/Sell/Trade, Links, Pictures

Wal Moreau
  http://www.moreau.com/
  General Information, Buy/Sell/Trade, Links, Pictures
www.antiqueguns.com
  http://www.antiqueguns.com/
  General Information, Buy/Sell/Trade, Links, Pictures

Related Publication Sites
The Enfield Collector's Digest
  http://www.ptialaska.net/~akenfhq/
Gun Journal
  http://www.shooters.com/gunjournal/

Western Americana

World Wide Web
Globalarts.com
  http://www.globalarts.com/
  Buy/Sell/Trade, Links, Pictures
www.antiqueguns.com
  http://www.antiqueguns.com/
  General Information, Buy/Sell/Trade, Links, Pictures

America Online
Message Board:
  GO ANTIQUE, select antiques & memorabilia M-Z, select western/ranch/farm items

Women's Items

World Wide Web
A Wink & A Smile
  http://rampages.onramp.net/~wnksmile/
  Buy/Sell/Trade, Links, Pictures
The Bee's Knee
  http://www.biddeford.com/~tbkkpt/
  Buy/Sell/Trade
Depression Delights
  http://www.main.com/~dd/
  Buy/Sell/Trade, Links, Pictures
Montage - The Perfume Bottle Information Center
  http://www.cicat.com/montage/
  General Information, Buy/Sell/Trade, Links, Pictures
Reflections of the Past
  http://www.victoriana.com/antiques/
  Buy/Sell/Trade, Pictures

America Online
Message Board:
GO ANTIQUE, select antiques & memorabilia M-Z, select hat pin/antique vanity

World's Fair & Expos

World Wide Web
A Sentimental Journey
http://www.rapidramp.com/Users/sjourney/
General Information, Buy/Sell/Trade, Links
ANTKonLINE
http://www.suba.com/ANTKonLINE/
Buy/Sell/Trade, Links, Pictures
Raymond's Antiques
http://www.collectors-row.com/raymonds-antiques/index.html
Buy/Sell/Trade
Way Out West Antiques
http://www.wayoutwest.com/
Buy/Sell/Trade, Pictures

Help Us Stay Up-to-Date in Cyberspace

The Internet is an ever-growing and constantly changing communication medium. By the time this book is printed, some collector-related sites listed here will have disappeared, and other new ones will be available.

You can help update our listings for the next annual edition. We would really like to hear from you regarding:

- Sites listed in this book that are no longer available
- Existing sites with URL addresses that have changed
- New sites that may be of special interest to collectors

We also invite you to visit us online to vote for what you feel is the best all-around site in your area of collecting. We plan to include a "Reader's Choice" section in our next edition, and your favorite site may make that list!

Contact us at either of these online addresses to keep us up-to-date:

http://www.csmonline.com/cyberspace
or
http://www.collect.com/cyberspace

Glossary

America Online (AOL): An on-line service provider.

ASCII (American Standard Code for Information Interchange): A standard encoding of characters widely used in the computer industry.

Bounce, bounced: E-mail being returned because it couldn't be delivered.

Browser: A program, typically used to "browse the Web," that allows a person to read hypertext. Netscape, Mosaic, Lynx and W3 are examples of browsers for the World Wide Web.

CompuServe Information Service (CIS): One of the services run by CompuServe Corporation. CIS provides a wide variety of on-line information services.

Cyberspace: The "universe" containing computers, programs and data.

Database: Large structured set(s) of data.

Domain name: The name of the system or Internet provider.

Download/upload: To transfer data from one computer to another. (You download to your computer, upload to another computer.)

Electronic mail (e-mail): Messages automatically passed from one computer user to another, often through computer networks and/or via modems over telephone lines.

FAQ: Refers to a document containing frequently asked questions and their answers.

Flame: A strong opinion or criticism of something in an electronic mail message. "Flame wars" happen when people start flaming each other back and forth.

FTP (file transfer protocol): Allows you to share files with another computer. Using FTP, you can download or upload between your computer and another. Sometimes, you may be asked to logon to an FTP site. If you do not have a user ID and password, try entering ANONYMOUS at the login name and your e-mail address as the password. Often, this will work and is called "anonymous FTP."

Home page or Homepage: The main document for a collection of linked sites on the Internet (like the table of contents for a book).

HTML (hyper text markup language): The programming language used to make World Wide Web pages. It defines the functions to be performed when you click on a button, image or hypertext on a page.

HTTP (hyper text transport protocol): The method by which the World Wide Web provides hypertext links between Web pages—often located on entirely different machines. To reach a hypertext document on the Web, you need to begin the address with "HTTP."

Hypertext: Text that links the user to another document or site.

Information Superhighway: High-speed global communications network (such as the Internet).

Internaut: Someone who uses the Internet.

KB (kilobyte): 1,024 bytes.

Lynx: A World Wide Web browser.

MB (megabyte): 1,024 kilobytes or 1,048,5765 bytes.

Modem: An electronic device that connects one computer to another via telephone lines.

Mosaic: A World Wide Web browser.

Navigating: Finding your way around, particularly on the World Wide Web. A browser is a tool for navigating hypertext documents.

Netiquette: A pun on the word "etiquette." It refers to proper behavior for users of the Internet.

Netscape Navigator: A World Wide Web browser.

Newgroups: Collections of articles (e-mail messages, questions, documents, etc.) arranged by topic and distributed to computers all over the Internet.

Prodigy: A commercial on-line conferencing service.

Protocol: A system of rules and procedures governing communications between two devices.

Server: A computer dedicated to providing specific services to client computers.

Shareware: Computer software that users can try before they buy. Users are asked to evaluate the software for a specified or indefinite period of time, and then either discontinue use or submit payment of a specific sum of money to the author of the software as "registration." Failure to pay the requested fee is a legal violation of the author's copyright rights.

Snail mail: Slang for mail sent via the U.S. Postal Service.

TCP/IP (Transmission Control Protocol/Internet Protocol): The basic protocol used to connect machines on the Internet is referred to as the Internet Protocol or IP. The Transmission Control Protocol (TCP) interacts with IP to provide an application protocol interface. The term has come to generically refer to a family of protocols used to connect local area networks to one another, forming an internet, more specifically, the global internetwork, referred to as the Internet.

URL (Uniform Resource Locator): A system of references to different Internet resources, indicating the type of protocol or application program used to reach it, the site and the specific resource.

Usenet (users' network): A "message bulletin board" system on which people can post and read articles (questions, opinions, etc.). To join, you need a news reader (software that is included with most Web browsers). Not all Internet service providers subscribe to Usenet and not all Usenet hosts (groups) are on the Internet, but there is a large overlap.

USPS: U.S. Postal Service.

Virus: A program that replicates itself on computer systems by incorporating itself into other programs that are shared among computer users. Most often, you receive a computer virus by downloading a program from another computer and then executing it. Equip your computer with good (and up-to-date) virus-checking software and don't download from a site that you don't trust.

World Wide Web (WWW, W3, the Web): A network of graphical hypertext servers linked by the Internet. It offers graphics, sound, text and other information.

WYSIWYG: An acronym for what you see is what you get.

ZIP: File extension for files compressed using the PKZIP compression utilities.

start now

click here

http://www.csmonline.com

sell, trade, or buy pieces for your collection   **CLASSIFIEDS**

shop for that one-of-a-kind antique   **MALL STORES**

look for shows, auctions & events   **CALENDARS**

access reference books & price guides   **BOOKS**

connect with other buyers & sellers   **MAGAZINES**

search our current, online price guide   **PRICE GUIDE**

locate local dealers, auctioneers, & appraisers   **DIRECTORIES**

talk with other collectors around the world   **FORUMS**

stay in touch with market news & trends   **NEWS**

receive all kinds of free stuff   **FREE STUFF**

the largest online source of information & merchandise for collectors

Collector's Super Mall

http://www.csmonline.com or http://www.collect.com

CSM OnLine For more information about CSM OnLine, e-mail to webmaster@csmonline.com or call 1-800-482-3158